A BIBLE VERSE EACH DAY

Food for the Soul: 365+ Meditations to Counsel, Cheer and Comfort

Jo Johnson

Copyright © 2025 by Jo Johnson

All rights reserved.

No part of this book may be reproduced in any form or by any electronic or mechanical means, including information storage and retrieval systems, without written permission from the author, except for the use of brief quotations in a book review.

Paperback Edition, First Printing, 2025

ISBN 978-1-7397443-6-6

Rosebine Press
6 Rosebine Gardens
Glenrothes
United Kingdom
KY76HG

rosebinepress@yahoo.com
www.rosebinepress.com

Cover Photo © 2025 by Jo Johnson:
The Quiraing, Isle of Skye, Scotland.

Copyright Acknowledgements

English Standard Version
Scripture quotations marked (ESV) are from the ESV® Bible (The Holy Bible, English Standard Version®), copyright © 2001 by Crossway, a publishing ministry of Good News Publishers. Used by permission. All rights reserved.

King James Version
Scripture quotations marked (KJV) are from The Authorized (King James) Version. Rights in the Authorized Version in the United Kingdom are vested in the Crown. Reproduced by permission of the Crown's patentee, Cambridge University Press.

New American Standard Bible
Scripture quotations marked (NASB) are taken from the New American Standard Bible® (NASB), Copyright © 1960, 1962, 1963, 1968, 1971, 1972, 1973, 1975, 1977, 1995 by The Lockman Foundation Used by permission. www.Lockman.org

New International Version
Scripture quotations marked (NIV) are taken from the Holy Bible, New International Version®, NIV®. Copyright © 1973, 1978, 1984, 2011 by Biblica, Inc.TM Used by permission of Zondervan. All rights reserved worldwide. www.zondervan.comThe 'NIV' and 'New International Version' are trademarks registered in the United States Patent and Trademark Office by Biblica, Inc.TM

New King James Version
Scripture quotations marked (NKJV) are taken from the New King James Version®. Copyright © 1982 by Thomas Nelson. Used by permission. All rights reserved.

New Living Translation
Scripture quotations marked (NLT) are taken from the Holy Bible, New Living Translation, copyright ©1996, 2004, 2015 by Tyndale House Foundation. Used by permission of Tyndale House Publishers, a Division of Tyndale House Ministries, Carol Stream, Illinois 60188. All rights reserved.

Revised Version
Scripture quotations marked (RV) are taken from the English Revised Version, 1885. The text of this Bible is in the public domain.

In compliance with 'fair use' policies, no more than 25% of any Bible version or 25% of any book therein, has been quoted in this work.

Image Credits
Chapter heading images provided by Pixabay (https://pixabay.com) under the Creative Commons Zero (CC0) license ("CC0 Content").

Contents

Foreword	ix
1. Atoning Blood	1
2. Abundance	3
3. Adoption	5
4. The Christian's Armour	7
5. Asking in Faith	9
6. The Authority of Christ	11
7. Baptism	13
8. Betrayal and Injustice	15
9. Born from Above: The New Birth	17
10. Christ's Perfection and Beauty	19
11. The Character of God	27
12. Children	31
13. Comfort	33
14. Compassion	35
15. Commitment	39
16. Communion	43
17. Courage	45
18. The New Covenant	49
19. Crisis Times	53
20. The Death of Christ	59
21. Decision Making and Change	63
22. The Deity of Christ	67
23. Dependence	73
24. Deliverance from Depression	79
25. Devotion	81
26. Difficulty	85
27. Divine Guidance and Direction	87
28. Divine Judgement	91
29. Divine light	93

30. Divine Perspective and Divine Power	97
31. Divine Protection and Divine Care	103
32. Election, Freewill and Sovereign Grace	107
33. Encouragement	111
34. The End of this Present World	113
35. Eternal view	115
36. Evil	121
37. Excuses	123
38. The Exaltation of Christ	125
39. Eyewitnesses of His Majesty	127
40. Falling Short	129
41. Personal Faith	133
42. Walking by Faith	143
43. Faithfulness	147
44. Fear	149
45. Fruitbearing	151
46. Freedom from the Power of Sin	153
47. Forgiveness	155
48. Giving God the First Place in Our Heart	159
49. God's Priorities	165
50. Good News!	167
51. Grace	171
52. Greed	175
53. Guidance	177
54. The Holy Spirit	179
55. Hypocrisy	181
56. Humility	183
57. The House of God	189
58. Holiness	191
59. Injustice and Betrayal	193
60. Integrity	195
61. Righteous Judgement	197
62. Justice	205
63. Justification	207
64. The Coming King	211
65. Kindness And Generosity	219

66. Kingdom, Christ's Millennial kingdom	223
67. Laziness	227
68. The Light of Life	229
69. Living Water	231
70. Divine Love	235
71. Sacrificial Love	239
72. Love of The World	245
73. Loyalty	247
74. Mercy	249
75. Music: Of Heaven and of Men	251
76. Obedience	253
77. Patience	259
78. Peace	261
79. Prayer	263
80. Praise, Thanksgiving and Thankfulness	267
81. The Priesthood of Christ	271
82. Human Pride	273
83. Promise	275
84. Divine Providence	279
85. The Purposes of God	285
86. Reconciliation	289
87. Redemption	291
88. Repentance	295
89. Reward	301
90. Resurrection	305
91. Restoration	309
92. Righteousness	311
93. The Rock of Ages	317
94. Personal Sacrifice	319
95. Salvation	323
96. Sanctification	329
97. Eternal Security	331
98. Service	333
99. The Silence of The Lamb	335
100. Wilful Sin	337
101. Sowing the Good Seed	339

102. Spiritual Food		341
103. Spiritual Vision and Spiritual Blindness		343
104. Spiritual Wealth		345
105. Suffering and Persecution		349
106. The Suffering of Christ		355
107. Trees		361
108. Triumph and Victory		363
109. Truth and Sincerity		365
110. Unbelief		369
111. Unity		371
112. Vengeance		375
113. Wisdom		377
114. Worship		381
Bibliography		385
About the Author		387
Also by Jo Johnson		389

FOREWORD

I compiled these Bible verses and comments for 'Golden Bells'—a calendar of tear-off scripture readings published by *Hayes Press** between 2016 and 2022. Some of these verses spoke to my heart in times of personal challenge. I share them with you here in this more permanent form. There are more than 460 Bible verses followed by a short comment— enough to keep you going for a year and two months! I hope you may enjoy them as I have, and with the help of the Holy Spirit, use them as an aid to gathering precious thoughts of your own from the Bible's inexhaustible store of heavenly wisdom.

Jo Johnson, December 2024

---

* https://hayespress.org/

How to Use this Book

The readings may be used in different ways.

1. DAILY READINGS

The 114 chapter headings in the Contents pages are arranged in alphabetical order. You may choose to go through them chronologically, or just dip into subjects that 'speak' to you.

2. QUIET TIME STUDY NOTES

You might make notes in a separate study notebook, either as a springboard to further study, or as a personal journal, documenting how God is working in your life.

This old Sunday School chorus underlines the value of setting aside time for regular Bible reading:

> *There's no book like the Bible,*
> *God's precious Word of Truth;*
> *The comfort of the aged,*
> *The guide and guard of youth;*
> *We won't give up the Bible,*
> *Though others say we should,*
> *For they can never find us another half so good!*

∽

BLESSED IS THE PERSON WHO LISTENS TO ME, WATCHING DAILY AT MY GATES, WAITING AT MY DOORPOSTS.

— PROVERBS 8:34 NASB

Atoning Blood

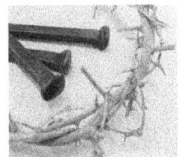

WHEN I SEE THE BLOOD, I WILL PASS OVER YOU....

— *Exodus 12:13 (RV)*

The blood of a lamb, an unblemished, sin atoning sacrifice, enabled the thrice Holy God of heaven to spare the children of Israel. Not because they were morally superior in any way to the Egyptians but because they placed their hopes in the God-given way of salvation: *'with precious blood as of a lamb without blemish and without spot...'* (1 Pet. 1:19)

A BIBLE VERSE EACH DAY

Like birds hovering overhead, the Lord Almighty will shield Jerusalem; he will shield it and deliver it, he will 'pass over' it and will rescue it.

— (Isaiah 31:5 NIV)

The Hebrew word *pawsach*, translated 'pass over' is also translated 'waver' or 'halt' as used by Elijah: *'how long will you waver between two opinions.'* (1 Kings 18;21) As birds hover over their young, so the Lord protects those who put their trust in Him: *'When I see the blood I will pass over you.'* (Ex. 12:13)

As high priest that year he prophesied that Jesus would die for the Jewish nation, and not only for that nation but also for the scattered children of God, to bring them together and make them one.

— (John 11:51,52 NIV)

Ellicott wrote: '[Caiaphas] …by his counsel and action in the Sanhedrin, was causing the sacrifice which should be presented by another high priest, in the Holy of Holies as an Atonement for the world—*'Christ being come an high priest of good things to come … by His own blood He entered in once into the holy place, having obtained eternal redemption'* (Hebrews 9:11-12).'

Abundance

WHEN HE HAD TAKEN THE SEVEN LOAVES AND GIVEN THANKS, HE BROKE THEM AND GAVE THEM TO HIS DISCIPLES TO DISTRIBUTE ... THE PEOPLE ATE AND WERE SATISFIED. AFTERWARD THE DISCIPLES PICKED UP SEVEN BASKETFULS OF BROKEN PIECES THAT WERE LEFT OVER.

— (MARK 8:6-8 NIV)

Seven loaves and a few fish. Four thousand well-fed people. Seven full baskets of leftovers. Our God is *'able to do exceeding abundantly above all that we ask or think.'* (Eph. 3:20 RV)

ADOPTION

I will say to those called 'Not my people,' 'You are my people'; and they will say, 'You are my God.'

— (Hosea 2:23 NIV)

P aul applies this verse to Gentile believers in Romans chapter 9. God will own both Jews and Gentiles as his people, when they put their trust in the righteousness of Christ and not in their own good works. *'the one who believes in him will never be put to shame.'* (Rom. 9:33)

The Christian's Armour

Stand firm then, with the belt of truth... breastplate of righteousness... feet fitted with...the gospel of peace...take up the shield of faith... the helmet of salvation and the sword of the Spirit, which is the word of God.

— (Ephesians 6:14-17 NIV)

This is the full armour of God for the disciple of Christ. It doesn't include *'the garments of vengeance'* (Isaiah 59:17), because these belong to the One who said: *'It is mine to avenge; I will repay'* (Deut. 32:35)

Asking in Faith

IF YOU THEN, THOUGH YOU ARE EVIL, KNOW HOW TO GIVE GOOD GIFTS TO YOUR CHILDREN, HOW MUCH MORE WILL YOUR FATHER IN HEAVEN GIVE THE HOLY SPIRIT TO THOSE WHO ASK HIM!

— (LUKE 11:13 NIV)

What will you ask for today? The Lord Jesus taught His disciples to ask Him to meet their daily needs, to forgive their sins against others and to keep them from falling prey to temptation. But He also encouraged them to *ask for the Holy Spirit*. As saved persons, believers on Jesus have the Holy Spirit indwelling them. When we give place to the old nature we become insensitive to the promptings of the Spirit. It is recorded of Stephen that he was FULL of the Holy Spirit. Our heavenly Father is just waiting for us to ask.

A BIBLE VERSE EACH DAY

MY FATHER WILL GIVE YOU WHATEVER YOU ASK IN MY NAME. UNTIL NOW YOU HAVE NOT ASKED FOR ANYTHING IN MY NAME. ASK AND YOU WILL RECEIVE, AND YOUR JOY WILL BE COMPLETE.

— (JOHN 16:23,24 NIV)

There are no limitations to God's power. God can do anything but fail! But He wants us to ask when we need help. When in Jesus name we acknowledge our dependence on Him, He will open the windows of heaven and pour us out a blessing.

The Authority of Christ

IN MY FORMER BOOK, THEOPHILUS, I WROTE ABOUT ALL THAT JESUS BEGAN TO DO AND TO TEACH.

— (ACTS 1:1 NIV)

The Lord's teaching was backed up by His deeds. What He did and what He said were not contradictory. The hypocritical Pharisees gave a mixed message - 'Do as we say, not as we do.' The words of the Lord Jesus had authority because they were backed up by His actions: *'he taught them as one who had authority, not as the teachers of the law.'* (Mark 1:22)

Baptism

For the wages of sin is death, but the free gift of God is eternal life in Christ Jesus our Lord.

— (Romans 6:23 ESV)

Paul makes this statement at the end of a discourse on the symbolism and the implications of believer's baptism. He reminds his audience that as Christ died and rose again, so they must die to their old way of life and live in the light and power of the eternal life which God has given them in Christ.

BETRAYAL AND INJUSTICE

MISERABLE COMFORTERS ARE YE ALL...MY FRIENDS SCORN ME

— (JOB 16:2,20 RV)

If Job felt let down by his friends, how much more did Judas' betrayal hurt the Lord Jesus? The words of King David prefigure His experience: *'If an enemy were insulting me, I could endure it; if a foe were rising against me, I could hide. But it is you, a man like myself, my companion, my close friend with whom I once enjoyed sweet fellowship at the house of God'* (Ps 55:12,13)

∼

A BIBLE VERSE EACH DAY

AND THEY WEIGHED OUT AS MY WAGES THIRTY
PIECES OF SILVER ... SO I TOOK THE THIRTY PIECES
OF SILVER AND THREW THEM INTO THE HOUSE OF
THE LORD, TO THE POTTER.

— (ZECH. 11:12,13 ESV)

Thirty pieces of silver
Laid in Iscariot's hand;
Thirty pieces of silver
And the aid of an arméd band,
Like a lamb that is led to the slaughter, Brought
   the humbled Son of God
At midnight, from the garden
Where His sweat had been like blood.

— (W. BLANE)

~

YOU...SMEAR ME WITH LIES; YOU ARE WORTHLESS
PHYSICIANS, ALL OF YOU! IF ONLY YOU WOULD BE
ALTOGETHER SILENT! FOR YOU, THAT WOULD BE
WISDOM.

— (JOB 13:4,5 NIV)

Thus Job replied to the continual and unfair criticism of those who were supposed to be his 'friends'! The story is told of a Scotsman who slipped out of a church service early. On his way down the steps of the Kirk a passing friend asked, *'Is he finished?'* To which he replied *'Aye, he's finished but he'll no' stop.'* There are times when 'less is more'!

Born from Above: The New Birth

TO THOSE WHO BELIEVED IN HIS NAME, HE GAVE
THE RIGHT TO BECOME CHILDREN OF GOD.

— (JOHN 1:12 NIV)

Belief in *'his name'* is the basis upon which a person becomes a child of God. By faith—by acknowledging that Jesus Christ, who is God in human form, is the true light. He alone has the authority and power to give me spiritual light and life. Through Him I can be reborn, into an eternal, family relationship with God.

Christ's Perfection and Beauty

HAVE THEM MAKE AN ARK OF ACACIA WOOD.

— (Exodus 25:10 NIV)

Acacia (from a Hebrew word meaning to pierce or flog) - an extremely durable, almost incorruptible wood. Yet it grows in the desert unseen by most. The incorruptible beauty of the Lord Jesus was not hidden from His God and Father. *'He grew up before him as a tender plant, and as a root out of a dry ground'* (Isaiah 53) He was flogged by Pilate; at the cross, His hands and feet were pierced by the nails and his side with a spear; Christ, the perfect man, suffered all this for me.

A BIBLE VERSE EACH DAY

I DELIGHT TO DO YOUR WILL, O MY GOD; YOUR LAW IS WITHIN MY HEART.

— (PSALM 40:8 NIV)

The law of the ten commandments was kept unbroken in two places only – in the ark of the covenant (the type), and in the person of the Lord Jesus Christ (the antitype). He came to Calvary in all the strength of that unbroken law, in the strength of One who fulfilled it in the spirit as well as the letter.

> *In Him the shadows of the law*
> *Are all fulfilled and now withdraw.*
>
> — THOMAS KELLY

Christ's Perfection and Beauty

GRACE IS POURED UPON YOUR LIPS.

— Psalm 45:2 ESV

All...were amazed at the gracious words that came from his lips.

— Luke 4:22 NIV

all the people hung on his words.

— Luke 19:48 NIV

No-one ever spoke like the Lord Jesus! He was the Living Word and He opened up the scriptures as none other could. No wonder crowds of people *'hung upon him'*, listening intently to every word. Even the officers sent to arrest Him said *'No one ever spoke the way this man does'* (John 7:46) Today we hear His voice as we read and meditate upon God's Holy Word.

A BIBLE VERSE EACH DAY

I OFFERED MY BACK TO THOSE WHO BEAT ME, MY CHEEKS TO THOSE WHO PULLED OUT MY BEARD; I DID NOT HIDE MY FACE FROM MOCKING AND SPITTING.

— ISAIAH 50:6 NIV

In majestic meekness He offered His back to those who beat Him; His cheeks to the malevolent men who tore the hair from His beard. He did not retaliate. The very silence of the gentle, Holy Lamb of God condemned their vile actions and speaks so loudly even now, of the grace and mercy that our Saviour showed toward rebellious sinners.

I NEED TO BE BAPTIZED BY YOU …

— MAT. 3:13 NKJV

John, Jesus earthly cousin, knew more about Him than most. He knew this person had never put a foot wrong. He knew Jesus was completely devoted to the things of God. He knew His righteousness was on a different level from all others. There was no hypocrisy, no inconsistency, no saying one thing and doing another with Jesus. He was absolutely straight as a die, upright in all His ways.

CHRIST'S PERFECTION AND BEAUTY

NOW I, PAUL, MYSELF AM PLEADING WITH YOU BY THE MEEKNESS AND GENTLENESS OF CHRIST ...

— 2 COR 10:1 NKJV

Disciples of Christ are followers of the Lamb of God. To Him belongs all authority in heaven and on earth, yet His character is 'meek and gentle'. This is foreign to human nature. We must enrol in His school and *learn* to be like Him. *'Take my yoke upon you, and learn from me, for I am gentle and lowly in heart, and you will find rest for your souls.'* (Mat. 11:29 NKJV)

LET US RUN WITH PERSEVERANCE THE RACE MARKED OUT FOR US, FIXING OUR EYES ON JESUS, THE PIONEER AND PERFECTER OF FAITH

— HEBREWS 12:1,2 NIV

The 'pioneer' (elsewhere translated 'author'), means the founder and leader - the one who by His own perfect example 'blazed the trail', and opened up the way into God's presence for us. In Him our faith will be perfected, finished, completed - it will not be found wanting because through His atoning death He removed every barrier to our acceptance by a thrice holy God. Praise His Name!

A BIBLE VERSE EACH DAY

HIS FACE LIKE LIGHTNING, HIS EYES LIKE FLAMING TORCHES, HIS ARMS AND LEGS LIKE THE GLEAM OF BURNISHED BRONZE, AND HIS VOICE LIKE THE SOUND OF A MULTITUDE.

— Dan. 10:6 NIV

HIS EYES WERE LIKE BLAZING FIRE. HIS FEET WERE LIKE BRONZE GLOWING IN A FURNACE, AND HIS VOICE WAS LIKE THE SOUND OF RUSHING WATERS...HIS FACE WAS LIKE THE SUN SHINING IN ALL ITS BRILLIANCE.

— Rev. 1:14,15,16 NIV

'Who is He...?
'Tis the Lord! oh wondrous story!
'Tis the Lord! the King of glory!
At His feet we humbly fall,
  Crown Him! crown Him, Lord of all!'

Christ's Perfection and Beauty

> As soon as Jesus was baptized, he went up out of the water...And a voice from heaven said, 'This is my Son, whom I love; with him I am well pleased.'
>
> — Mat. 3:16,17 NIV

The Lord Jesus had no sin. He didn't need to publicly demonstrate dying to sin and rising to walk in a new way of life. But His baptism foreshadowed the purpose for which He came to earth--to die for your sins and mine, and to rise from the dead, mighty to save. No wonder God expressed such delight in His beloved Son.

> One of the criminals who hung there hurled insults at him: 'Aren't you the Messiah? Save yourself and us!' But the other criminal rebuked him. 'Don't you fear God...? We are punished justly, for we are getting what our deeds deserve. But this man has done nothing wrong.'
>
> — Luke 23:39-41 NIV

The first criminal died with *sin in him and on him*; The second criminal died with *sin in him but not on him*; The perfect man who died on the middle cross had *sin on him but not in him* because as the Lamb of God, He was 'taking away the sin of the world.' (John 1:29 YLT)

A BIBLE VERSE EACH DAY

Now I, Paul, myself am pleading with you by the meekness and gentleness of Christ ...

— 2 Cor 10:1 NKJV

Disciples of Christ are followers of the Lamb of God. To Him belongs all authority in heaven and on earth, yet His character is 'meek and gentle'. This is foreign to human nature. We must enrol in His school and *learn* to be like Him. *'Take my yoke upon you, and learn from me, for I am gentle and lowly in heart, and you will find rest for your souls.'* (Mat. 11:29 NKJV)

∽

The Character of God

THE EARTH IS FULL OF THE LOVINGKINDNESS OF THE LORD.

— (Psalm 33:5 R.V.)

We don't have to look far to see this truth. Look at the way parent birds care for and rear their young, constantly flying back and forth to bring them food; look at the prolific growth that cultivated soil produces, giving abundant harvests and the fragrance and beauty of flowers. How grateful we should be to God, who gives us *'life and breath and all things'* (Acts 17:25).

A BIBLE VERSE EACH DAY

Have mercy upon me, O God, according to thy lovingkindness: according unto the multitude of thy tender mercies blot out my transgressions.

— Psalm 51:1 KJV

The only thing that draws the soul to seek the face of God is 'the loving-kindness of God, the multitude of his tender mercies.' It is a look at Calvary; a sight of the face of Jesus which alone can draw our back-slidden heart to cry, *'Have mercy upon me.'*

R.M. McCheyne, 1841

∽

The grass withers and the flowers fall, but the word of our God endures forever.

— *Isaiah 40:8 (NIV)*

In contrast with the transient nature of things in this world, the living word of our omnipresent, omniscient, omnipotent, God, never dies.

omnipresent = *present everywhere at the same time*
omniscient = *simultaneously seeing everything, everywhere*
omnipotent = *having supreme authority and power over everything and everyone.*

∽

JESUS SAID: 'HEAVEN AND EARTH WILL PASS AWAY,
BUT MY WORDS WILL NEVER PASS AWAY'

— MAT. 24:25

ALL THINGS HAVE BEEN DELIVERED TO ME BY MY
FATHER, AND NO ONE KNOWS THE SON EXCEPT THE
FATHER. NOR DOES ANYONE KNOW THE FATHER
EXCEPT THE SON, AND THE ONE TO WHOM THE SON
WILLS TO REVEAL HIM.

— MAT. 11:27 (NKJV)

The Lord said to Philip, *'He who has seen me has seen the Father'* (John 14:9 NKJV) Many Jews refused to accept that the Lord Jesus was *'Immanuel'*, *'God with us'*. Jesus said *'I and the Father are one.'* (John 10:30 ESV). Only the eye of faith can see God the Father in the Son.

Children

If anyone causes one of these little ones—those who believe in me—to stumble, it would be better for them to have a large millstone hung around their neck and to be drowned in the depths of the sea.

— *Mat. 18:6 (NIV)*

The Lord Jesus made it very clear that those who corrupt the minds of the young are guilty of a monstrous crime. People who teach children to turn away from the wholesome values of God's Word will answer to Him for their actions.

Comfort

Job's three friends...sat with him on the ground seven days and seven nights, and no one spoke a word to him, for they saw that his suffering was very great.

— *Job 2:11,13 (ESV)*

The sympathetic silence of Job's three friends was more eloquent and comforting than their words. Unfortunately, when they opened their mouths, they spoiled the effect. Sometimes our presence is the best comfort we can give to those whose suffering is beyond human comprehension.

Compassion

And the LORD said, 'You pity the plant, for which you did not labour...And should not I pity Nineveh, that great city...?'

— *Jonah 4:10,11 (ESV)*

God cared about what Jonah felt and thought! God wanted his servant to develop a world vision, to mirror in some measure, His compassion for lost souls. He wants us to see the bigger picture too.

A BIBLE VERSE EACH DAY

And should not I pity Nineveh, that great city, in which there are more than 120,000 persons who do not know their right hand from their left, and also much cattle?

— Jonah 4:11 (ESV)

'He prayeth well who loveth well
Both man and bird and beast.
He prayeth best who loveth best
All things, both great and small:
For the dear God who loveth us,
He made and loveth all.'

— from 'The Ancient Mariner', by Samuel T. Coleridge.

If any of you has a sheep and it falls into a pit on the Sabbath, will you not take hold of it and lift it out? How much more valuable is a person than a sheep! Therefore it is lawful to do good on the Sabbath.

— Matt 12:11,12 (NIV)

Incontrovertible logic! Not one of them would have left a valuable sheep to die in a well on the Sabbath - if a sheep was worth rescuing, how much more valuable the life of a man, made in the image of God?

Compassion

> AND JESUS IN PITY TOUCHED THEIR EYES, AND IMMEDIATELY THEY RECOVERED THEIR SIGHT AND FOLLOWED HIM.
>
> — *MAT. 20:34 (ESV)*

Jesus led by example. If I want to be a great disciple of Christ, I'll need to learn to serve others the way He did. He had just revealed the secret of true greatness – *'whoever would be great among you must be your servant'* (v26). He then demonstrated this when He was moved with compassion by two blind men. Our Lord never ignored a cry for mercy.

> AN EXPERT IN THE LAW ... ASKED JESUS, 'AND WHO IS MY NEIGHBOUR?' ... IN REPLY JESUS SAID 'A MAN WAS GOING DOWN FROM JERUSALEM TO JERICHO, WHEN HE WAS ATTACKED BY ROBBERS ... LEAVING HIM HALF DEAD ... BUT A SAMARITAN ... TOOK PITY ON HIM ... GO AND DO LIKEWISE'.
>
> — *LUKE 10:25-37 (NIV)*

Jews and Samaritans were enemies. In telling this story, Jesus confronted the deeply held prejudice of His Jewish audience. The lesson is clear: if God brings someone who is obviously in desperate need of our help, within our sphere of influence, He expects us to go to their aid, regardless of their political, religious, social or cultural identity. The royal law transcends all barriers: *'Love your neighbour as yourself.'* (Leviticus 19:18)

Commitment

IN EVERY WORK THAT HE BEGAN IN THE SERVICE OF THE HOUSE OF GOD, AND IN THE LAW, AND IN THE COMMANDMENTS, TO SEEK HIS GOD, HE DID IT WITH ALL HIS HEART, AND PROSPERED.

— 2 CHRON. 31:21 (KJV)

There is no more important work we can be engaged in, than the service of the house of God. If we are to prosper spiritually, or in any other sphere, we must do it wholeheartedly.

WHATEVER YOUR HAND FINDS TO DO,
DO IT WITH ALL YOUR MIGHT.
ECC. 9:10 (NIV)

> IF YOU REMAIN SILENT AT THIS TIME, RELIEF AND DELIVERANCE...WILL ARISE FROM ANOTHER PLACE... AND WHO KNOWS BUT THAT YOU HAVE COME TO YOUR ROYAL POSITION FOR SUCH A TIME AS THIS?
>
> — *ESTHER 4:14 (NIV)*

Esther's Uncle, Mordecai, spelled out the gravity of the situation and made her realise that God had placed her in a position of influence. Esther courageously put her life on the line and spoke out on behalf of God's people. At such times God looks to His servants on earth, to witness for Him whatever the cost.

> IF YOU WANT TO BE PERFECT, GO, SELL YOUR POSSESSIONS AND GIVE TO THE POOR, AND YOU WILL HAVE TREASURE IN HEAVEN. THEN COME, FOLLOW ME.
>
> — *MAT. 19:21 (NIV)*

Some exclusive golf clubs charge an exorbitant entrance fee but have a more modest annual subscription.

There is no entrance fee for salvation because Jesus has already paid that price for us with his blood -

but the annual subscription for disciples is: *everything we have.*

> *Love that transcends our highest powers*
> *Demands our heart, our life, our all.'*
>
> — *ISAAC WATTS*

Commitment

> They called the apostles in and had them flogged. Then they ordered them not to speak in the name of Jesus ... Day after day, in the temple courts and from house to house, they never stopped teaching and proclaiming the good news that Jesus is the Messiah.
>
> — *Acts 5:40-42 (NIV)*

Peter and the apostles had told the authorities *'we must obey God rather than men'* (v29). Despite a severe beating and a religious court order, that is what they did.

> So the Twelve gathered all the disciples together and said, 'It would not be right for us to neglect the ministry of the word of God in order to wait on tables.'
>
> — *Acts 6:2 (NIV)*

Leaders must lead. Ministers of the Word must minister the Word. Helpers must help. Each of us must devote ourself to the calling to which God has called us. We must not be deflected from the work He has given us to do.

Communion

I WILL SEEK HIM WHOM MY SOUL LOVES. I SOUGHT HIM, BUT FOUND HIM NOT.

— *SONG OF SONGS 3:2 (ESV)*

RETURN TO ME, SAYS THE LORD OF HOSTS, AND I WILL RETURN TO YOU, SAYS THE LORD OF HOSTS.

— *ZECH. 1:3 (ESV)*

By divine invitation, we can have the immense privilege of fellowship with the LORD of hosts - the self-existent, eternal, supreme being at whose disposal are the vast armies of heaven. As someone once said: *'If God seems far away, guess who moved?'*

A BIBLE VERSE EACH DAY

MANY SHALL COME FROM THE EAST AND WEST, AND SHALL SIT DOWN WITH ABRAHAM, AND ISAAC, AND JACOB, IN THE KINGDOM OF HEAVEN.

— *MAT. 8:11 (KJV)*

Sitting down together speaks of fellowship together, enjoying the company of others. One day all the redeemed will sit down with our Saviour and LORD at *'the marriage supper of the Lamb.'* (Rev 19:9) Sharing His company continually and for ever after. What a wonderful day that will be!

THEY TOOK NOTE THAT THESE MEN HAD BEEN WITH JESUS.

— *ACTS 4:13 (NIV)*

The disciples spent three and a half years in His company. His character, thoughts and teaching were deeply impressed upon their lives. Such daily 'quality time' with the Lord Jesus is essential if others are to see *'Christ in you, the hope of glory'*. (Col. 1:27)

Courage

So everyone who acknowledges me before men, I also will acknowledge before my Father who is in heaven, but whoever denies me before men, I also will deny before my Father who is in heaven.

— *Mat. 10:32,33 (ESV)*

Our Lord expects His disciples to nail their colours to the mast. Those who keep their mouths shut when they should speak up for the one who gave His life for them, will lose the joy of fellowship with the Father and with the Lord Jesus and in a coming day, may lose the reward promised to those who are not ashamed of the Saviour who gave His life for them *(see 1 Cor. 5:10 & 10:10-15)*.

THEY WERE AFRAID OF THE JEWISH LEADERS, WHO ALREADY HAD DECIDED THAT ANYONE WHO ACKNOWLEDGED THAT JESUS WAS THE MESSIAH WOULD BE PUT OUT OF THE SYNAGOGUE.

— *JOHN 9:22 (NIV)*

The miracle of a man born blind having his eyes opened, was a huge problem for Jewish leaders who had already made public their rejection of the Son of God. It took the courage of the man born blind, to stand up to them even though they excommunicated him: *'If this man were not from God he could do nothing.'* (John 9:33 NIV)

ABOUT MIDNIGHT PAUL AND SILAS WERE PRAYING AND SINGING HYMNS TO GOD, AND THE OTHER PRISONERS WERE LISTENING TO THEM.

— *ACTS 16:25 (NIV)*

They had had their clothes ripped off them; they had been severely beaten with rods; the flogging had laid 'many stripes' on their backs; They had been thrown like criminals into the darkest dungeon where their feet were shackled in the stocks - yet instead of complaining, they prayed and sang hymns to God! What a testimony!

Courage

But the following night the Lord stood by him and said, 'Be of good cheer, Paul; for as you have testified for Me in Jerusalem, so you must also bear witness at Rome'.

— *Acts 23:11 (NKJV)*

When we stand up for Jesus in a hostile world, He will stand by us and enable us to speak on His behalf. They could tie Paul's hands but they could never bind the Word of God.

I am coming soon. Hold on to what you have, so that no one will take your crown.

— *Rev. 3:11 (NIV)*

None of us can relax our vigilance in spiritual things. There is the ever-present danger that we lower our vision and become distracted by things that are not to our profit. His reward is reserved for those who 'hold fast' and refuse to let go of the doctrines and practices that He has revealed to us in His Word.

The New Covenant

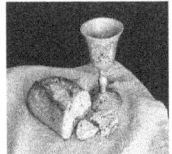

I SAY TO YOU THAT MANY WILL COME FROM THE EAST AND THE WEST, AND WILL TAKE THEIR PLACES AT THE FEAST WITH ABRAHAM, ISAAC AND JACOB IN THE KINGDOM OF HEAVEN.

— (MAT. 8:11 NIV)

Abraham, Isaac and Jacob - and many many more old covenant saints - lived by faith and because of Jesus death, will *'receive the promised eternal inheritance'* *(Heb 9:15)*. The *'many'* that *'will come from the east and the west'* to share that 'eternal inheritance' with them will be Gentiles like the Centurion in Matthew 8. Every one of them redeemed by Christ's blood under the new covenant. Praise God!

> NO ONE POURS NEW WINE INTO OLD WINESKINS. OTHERWISE, THE WINE WILL BURST THE SKINS, AND BOTH THE WINE AND THE WINESKINS WILL BE RUINED. NO, THEY POUR NEW WINE INTO NEW WINESKINS.
>
> — (MARK 2:22 NIV)

The new life that comes through faith in Christ cannot be accommodated within the old covenant tradition which was conditional on human obedience. The new creation *'in Christ'* (2 Cor. 5:17), requires a new covenant, validated by the blood of the eternal covenant —founded on Christ's perfect, unshakeable obedience.

~

> SO THOSE WHO RECEIVED HIS WORD WERE BAPTIZED... WERE ADDED ...AND THEY DEVOTED THEMSELVES TO THE APOSTLES' TEACHING AND THE FELLOWSHIP, TO THE BREAKING OF BREAD AND THE PRAYERS...
>
> — (ACTS 2:41,42 ESV)

There are no grey areas here. If we want to be at the centre of God's purposes we must go back to the original terms of the New Covenant as practised in these early days. The *'Israel of God'* (Gal 6:16), today are those who walk by faith and follow after 'the whole counsel of God' (Acts 20:27), not the imperfect traditions of men.

The New Covenant

It is my judgment, therefore, that we should not make it difficult for the Gentiles who are turning to God.

— (Acts 15:19 NIV)

When the leaders of the churches of God met to discuss whether Gentiles ought to be subject to rules regarding circumcision in the law of Moses, James, (the Lord's brother), gave this judgement. The majority agreed and divine unity was maintained.

He redeemed us in order that the blessing given to Abraham might come to the Gentiles through Christ Jesus...

— (Galatians 3:14 NIV)

'Christ became a curse for those who were cursed. He became a curse by dying upon a tree (Deut.21:22,23). Thus, not by law-keeping, in which there is no hope of salvation for the sinner, but by One who took man's place in death, by dying on the tree, the blessing of Abraham in Christ Jesus flows out to the Gentiles who were far off, and to the Jews who were nigh.'

(John Miller)

CRISIS TIMES

MOSES RETURNED TO THE LORD AND SAID, 'WHY, LORD, WHY HAVE YOU BROUGHT TROUBLE ON THIS PEOPLE? ... YOU HAVE NOT RESCUED YOUR PEOPLE AT ALL.'

— (Ex 5:22,23 NIV)

In the crisis of the moment, Moses forgot that God had forewarned him of Pharaoh's resistance. This was only the first stage in God's plan of redemption for Israel. We do well to remember that afflictions are but one stage in His purposes of grace for those who put their trust in Him.

THE LORD GAVE AND THE LORD HAS TAKEN AWAY;
MAY THE NAME OF THE LORD BE PRAISED.

— (JOB 1:21 NIV)

In one day Satan reduced Job's life-work to nothing. His wealth, possessions and family were all wiped out. But one thing Satan could not take away was Job's faith in God, which had matured during a lifetime of experience. Job had learned not to judge God *'by feeble sense'* but always to trust Him whose ways are higher than ours.

'God is his own interpreter and he shall make it plain' (PHSS 176), (William Cowper, 1731-1800)

IF YOU FAINT IN THE DAY OF ADVERSITY, YOUR STRENGTH IS SMALL.

— (PROVERBS 24:10 ESV)

Question: Where do we find the strength to keep going in times of distress?

Answer: *'From the ends of the earth I call to you, I call as my heart grows faint;* **lead me to the rock that is higher than I.***'* (Psalm 61:2)

CRISIS TIMES

> WHEN YOU PASS THROUGH THE WATERS, I WILL BE WITH YOU; AND WHEN YOU PASS THROUGH THE RIVERS, THEY WILL NOT SWEEP OVER YOU. WHEN YOU WALK THROUGH THE FIRE, YOU WILL NOT BE BURNED...
>
> — (ISAIAH 43:2 NIV)

Zarephath means 'refinery' as in the smelting of gold or silver. The intense heat burns off the dross and leaves the purified precious metal. Sometimes God turns up the heat in our lives to burn up the dross and get rid of the rubbish. He puts our faith to the test in such a way that our faith in Him becomes stronger.

> BEHOLD, I AM THE LORD, THE GOD OF ALL FLESH. IS ANYTHING TOO HARD FOR ME?
>
> — (JEREMIAH 32:27 NIV)

When the storms of life threaten to overwhelm, we *'take it to the Lord in prayer'*. Like Hezekiah did with the hostile letter he received, we should *'spread it before the LORD'.* (2 Kings 19:14-20...) But it's also great to know, *'Our God is so big, So strong and so Mighty, There's NOTHING that He cannot do!'*

THERE ARE THOSE WHO OPPRESS THE INNOCENT AND TAKE BRIBES AND DEPRIVE THE POOR OF JUSTICE IN THE COURTS. THEREFORE THE PRUDENT KEEP QUIET IN SUCH TIMES, FOR THE TIMES ARE EVIL.

— (AMOS 5:12,13 NIV)

In an evil time, those who are wise must carefully avoid the traps laid for them. In such circumstances, silently bringing the matter before the Lord is often the only way to go.

∼

HE GOT UP AND REBUKED THE WIND AND THE RAGING WATERS; THE STORM SUBSIDED, AND ALL WAS CALM. 'WHERE IS YOUR FAITH?' HE ASKED HIS DISCIPLES.

— (LUKE 8:24,25 NIV)

'His oath, His covenant, His blood,

Support me in the 'whelming flood;

When all around my soul gives way,

He then is all my Hope and Stay.'

— (EDWARD MOTE, 1797 - 1874)

∼

CRISIS TIMES

> BE FAITHFUL UNTO DEATH, AND I WILL GIVE YOU THE CROWN OF LIFE..
>
> — (REV 2:10 ESV)

Many Scottish Covenanters were killed because they refused to acknowledge that the King had a 'divine right' to override their conscience: James Renwick, whose only charge was that he frequently preached in the fields, was hanged at the Grassmarket in Edinburgh; John Brown was shot because he taught a Bible Class; Margaret MacLachlan and Margaret Wilson were drowned in the Solway Firth because they attended field meetings and house meetings for the worship of God instead of state approved Churches.

'He is no fool who gives what he cannot keep
to gain that which he cannot lose.'

Jim Elliot

They '...suffered the loss of all things...[to] gain Christ'
(Philippians 3:8)

I CRIED OUT TO THE LORD BECAUSE OF MY AFFLICTION, AND HE ANSWERED ME. 'OUT OF THE BELLY OF SHEOL I CRIED, AND YOU HEARD MY VOICE.

— (JONAH 2:2 NKJV)

Jonah's predicament was beyond his control. At such times, we are forcibly reminded that our lives are in God's hand. Like Jonah, we should cry out to the LORD for deliverance. He heard Jonah; He will hear our voice too.

∽

The Death of Christ

'He took her by the hand and said to her, 'Talitha koum!' (which means 'Little girl, I say to you, get up!'). Immediately the girl stood up and began to walk around...'

— Mark 5:41,42 NIV

The Lord Jesus has power over death. When all hope was gone, He restored Jairus's daughter to life. Praise God! He died to pay the price for our sins, and rose from the tomb, victorious over death, *'the firstfruits of them that are asleep.'* (1 Cor. 15:20)

> NOW ABOUT THE DEAD RISING—HAVE YOU NOT READ IN THE BOOK OF MOSES ... HOW GOD SAID TO HIM, 'I AM THE GOD OF ABRAHAM, THE GOD OF ISAAC, AND THE GOD OF JACOB'? HE IS NOT THE GOD OF THE DEAD, BUT OF THE LIVING.
>
> — MARK 12:26,27 NIV

People whose bodies have died are still alive to God. The story told by the Lord Jesus in Luke 16, about the rich man and Lazarus the beggar (who died and was carried by the angels to Abraham's bosom), provides further evidence confirming this striking statement.

> BUT IN THE ACCOUNT OF THE BURNING BUSH, EVEN MOSES SHOWED THAT THE DEAD RISE, FOR HE CALLS THE LORD 'THE GOD OF ABRAHAM, AND THE GOD OF ISAAC, AND THE GOD OF JACOB.' HE IS NOT THE GOD OF THE DEAD, BUT OF THE LIVING, FOR TO HIM ALL ARE ALIVE.
>
> — LUKE 20:37,38 NIV

The Lord made it very clear that everyone who dies has a continuing existence beyond the grave; those who die in faith are spiritually alive; for example, to the thief on the cross Jesus said: *'Today you will be with me in Paradise'*. (Luke 23:43) He's the God of the living!

The Death of Christ

The chief priests of the Jews protested to Pilate, 'Do not write 'The King of the Jews,' but that this man claimed to be king of the Jews.' Pilate answered, 'What I have written, I have written.'

— John 19:21,22 NIV

Peter put the sacrifice of the Lord Jesus Christ into perspective on the day of Pentecost:

'God raised him from the dead, freeing him from the agony of death, because it was impossible for death to keep its hold on him...God has made this Jesus, whom you crucified, both Lord and Messiah.' (Acts 2:24,35)

∼

We preach Christ crucified: a stumbling block to Jews and foolishness to Gentiles, but to those whom God has called, both Jews and Greeks, Christ the power of God and the wisdom of God.

— 1 Cor. 1:23,24 NIV

A crucified Messiah! God's way of salvation, through faith in His beloved Son, who offered Himself as a sacrifice to God for our sins, does not appeal to the natural mind, nor does it appeal to human pride. Only those who respond to God's call, discover the life-giving power that comes from our risen Lord.

∼

DECISION MAKING AND CHANGE

AND JEHOVAH SPAKE UNTO ME, SAYING, YE HAVE COMPASSED THIS MOUNTAIN LONG ENOUGH: TURN YOU NORTHWARD.

— DEUT. 2:2,3 RV

Sometimes we seem to be going round in circles, just 'marking time' spiritually. Perhaps we have to experience the plateau before higher things are possible. But when the voice of the Lord says 'enough!' - *'launch out into the deep'* (Luke 5:4, KJV), we discover that the Lord has richer blessings in store than we ever knew before.

> THE LORD IS WITH YOU WHEN YOU ARE WITH HIM.
> IF YOU SEEK HIM, HE WILL BE FOUND BY YOU, BUT IF
> YOU FORSAKE HIM, HE WILL FORSAKE YOU.
>
> — 2 CHRON. 15:1,2 NIV

God is scrupulously fair and righteous. If I seek the Lord I will find Him and He will be with me, will watch over me and bless me; but if I forsake Him and deliberately go my own way, I will suffer the consequences of my actions.

God is not in the business of forcing people to do His will - He looks for hearts that will respond to His love.

> SEEK THE LORD WHILE HE MAY BE FOUND; CALL ON
> HIM WHILE HE IS NEAR. LET THE WICKED FORSAKE
> THEIR WAYS AND THE UNRIGHTEOUS THEIR
> THOUGHTS. LET THEM TURN TO THE LORD, AND HE
> WILL HAVE MERCY ON THEM, AND TO OUR GOD, FOR
> HE WILL FREELY PARDON.
>
> — ISAIAH 55:6,7 NIV

This suggests that there is a time to respond to the voice of God; that it is possible for a person to resist the voice of God until God gives them up. This is too awful to contemplate. *'now is the time of God's favour, now is the day of salvation.'* (2 Cor 6:2 NIV)

Decision Making and Change

> PILATE... WASHED HIS HANDS... 'I AM INNOCENT OF THIS MAN'S BLOOD,' HE SAID...BUT HE HAD JESUS FLOGGED, AND HANDED HIM OVER TO BE CRUCIFIED.
>
> — MATT 27:24-26 NIV

There was no neutral option for Pilate - no sitting on the fence - he had to come down on one side or the other. His actions belied his words. There's no neutral option for us either. We must declare ourselves either for or against Jesus Christ the Son of God. Our actions in relation to the Saviour of sinners, will either accuse or excuse us.

> AND AS HE PASSED BY, HE SAW LEVI THE SON OF ALPHAEUS SITTING AT THE TAX BOOTH, AND HE SAID TO HIM, 'FOLLOW ME'. AND HE ROSE AND FOLLOWED HIM. — Mark 2:14 ESV

For Matthew Levi, the call of Jesus the Messiah, whose kingdom will last forever, was of infinitely more importance than anything else in the world. Mark 2:14 ESV

I heard Him call, 'Come, follow,' That was all.
My gold grew dim, my soul went after Him
I rose and followed, that was all.
Who would not follow if they heard Him call?

— H.W. LONGFELLOW

A BIBLE VERSE EACH DAY

MANY CAME TO HIM AT HIS LODGING, TO WHOM HE EXPLAINED AND SOLEMNLY TESTIFIED OF THE KINGDOM OF GOD, PERSUADING THEM CONCERNING JESUS FROM BOTH THE LAW OF MOSES AND THE PROPHETS, FROM MORNING TILL EVENING. AND SOME WERE PERSUADED BY THE THINGS WHICH WERE SPOKEN, AND SOME DISBELIEVED.

— ACTS 28:23,24 NKJV

God doesn't force people to become Christians. We are autonomous, rational beings with the ability to accept or reject the gospel message. But each of us will bear responsibility for the eternal consequences of the decision we make.

The Deity of Christ

'Simon Peter replied, 'You are the Christ, the Son of the living God.' And Jesus answered him, '...flesh and blood has not revealed this to you, but my Father who is in heaven...on this rock I will build my church, and the gates of hell shall not prevail against it.'

— Mat. 16:16-18 ESV

On this rock - not on Peter (a stone or boulder) - but upon the massive rock-solid foundation of His deity - on the Divinely revealed truth that Jesus is the Christ the Son of the living God - Christ would build His glorious, unassailable, impregnable, church, *'the church which is his body'* (Eph. 1:22-23).

'WHAT DO YOU THINK ABOUT THE MESSIAH? WHOSE SON IS HE?' 'THE SON OF DAVID,' THEY REPLIED.'

— MAT. 22:42 NIV

I t's not what you know but who you know that matters. Do you know Christ as more than the historical 'son of David'? Do you know him as the Son of God who became an offering for your sins on the cross? Do you know Him as Immanuel (God with us), who came down from heaven and died because he loved you? Do you know him as your Saviour?

'WHO IS THIS? EVEN THE WIND AND THE WAVES OBEY HIM!'

— MARK 4:41 NIV

T he Lord Jesus Christ could sleep through the storm because He made the wind and the waves. The elements were subject to His authority. Whatever happened, He was in complete control. Such incidents simply revealed who He was and is: God in human form.

The Deity of Christ

> 'Then they all said, 'Are You then the Son of God?' So He said to them, 'You rightly say that I am.''
>
> — Luke 22:70 NKJV

The Jews condemned the Lord Jesus because He identified Himself as co-equal with God. His astonishing miracles, which included raising the dead, proved His divine credentials beyond doubt. Yet they rejected Him. One day, they will answer to God for the choice they made—as will each one of us.

> 'We have found the Messiah'.
>
> — John 1:41 NIV

What a discovery! To recognise Jesus as the promised Saviour and King of Israel was one thing. It took some of His disciples longer to realise He was also God Incarnate. But the more they heard His teaching and witnessed His mighty works, the more they were convinced He was the Son of God from heaven.

"'Before Philip called you, when you were under the fig tree, I saw you.' Nathanael answered him, 'Rabbi, you are the Son of God! You are the King of Israel!'"

— John 1:48-49 ESV

Immediately Nathanael realised that only God could possibly have known what he was thinking, reading, praying, under the fig tree.

All his reservations were swept away: he bowed his heart before the incarnate Word, gladly acknowledging Him as the true Messiah—*'Son of God'* and *'King of Israel'*.

∼

'If I then, the Lord and the Master, have washed your feet, ye also ought to wash one another's feet.'

— John 13:14 RV

No matter how low He stooped - whether asleep in a boat, sitting beside a well, kneeling to wash the disciples feet, or standing before Pontius Pilate, He was always *'the Lord and the Master'*:

> *'Never can He yield His claim*
> *To those ever glorious words*
> *King of Kings and Lord of Lords'*

∼

The Deity of Christ

> 'I AND THE FATHER ARE ONE ... THE FATHER IS IN ME, AND I IN THE FATHER.'
>
> — John 10:26-39 RV

How can our finite minds begin to comprehend the profundity of this truth? The indivisible unity of Deity, the Triune God. And to then contemplate what took place at Golgotha, the place of a skull, the great intersection of divine grace and divine judgement, where God the Father laid our sins on God the Son.

How can we even begin to understand how God the Father could forsake God the Son, yet remain one indivisible, eternal unity? It is an impenetrable mystery which goes far beyond the ability of the human mind to understand.

All we know is that a profound, unique, never to be repeated event took place, where God the Father, God the Holy Spirit and God the Son dealt once and for all, with the devastating wickedness of sin in all its forms; and, that it cost our Saviour anguish beyond our comprehension.

Dependence

'And he humbled you and let you hunger and fed you with manna, ...that he might make you know that man does not live by bread alone, but man lives by every word that comes from the mouth of the LORD.'

— Deut 8:3 ESV

God allowed Israel to experience hunger and become totally dependent on His provision and on His leading and direction, so that they would learn that their life, health and wellbeing came from something more than their next crust of bread. They had to learn that the Word of God was the source of their life and health, individually and collectively, physically, morally and spiritually.

A BIBLE VERSE EACH DAY

'...LET HIM CURSE, FOR THE LORD HAS TOLD HIM TO. IT MAY BE THAT THE LORD WILL LOOK UPON MY MISERY AND RESTORE TO ME HIS COVENANT BLESSING INSTEAD OF HIS CURSE TODAY.'

— 2 SAMUEL 16:11,12 NIV

When wrongfully oppressed, those who trust in God don't take the law into their own hands. When they are treated shamefully they follow David's example and look to the Lord. He will defend and deliver those who put their trust in Him.

HELP US, LORD OUR GOD, FOR WE RELY ON YOU...LORD, YOU ARE OUR GOD; DO NOT LET MERE MORTALS PREVAIL AGAINST YOU.

— 2 CHRON. 14:11 NIV

Dependence

*'I lift up my eyes to the mountains
where does my help come from?
My help comes from the Lord,
the Maker of heaven and earth...
The Lord watches over you...
The Lord will keep you from all
harm...'*

— Ps. 121:1,2,5,7 NIV

'Those who know your name trust in you, for you, Lord, have never forsaken those who seek you.'

— Psalm 9:10

The Hebrew word for 'seek' has the thought of frequently seeking to or going to a place.

This is our experience in times of trial, when we can do no other but acknowledge our human weakness and our need of his strength. At such times we need to go often to *'the throne of grace 'to receive mercy and...find grace to help us in time of need.'* (Heb. 4:16)

A BIBLE VERSE EACH DAY

'How hard it is for the rich to enter the kingdom of God!' The disciples were amazed at his words. But Jesus said again, 'Children, how hard it is to enter the kingdom of God! It is easier for a camel to go through the eye of a needle than for someone who is rich to enter the kingdom of God.'

— Mark 10:23-25 NIV

The disciples were not spiritually mature enough to understand what the Lord was telling them. That's why He called them 'children'. Rich people tend to trust in their wealth instead of God.

'Simon's mother-in-law was in bed with a fever, and they immediately told Jesus about her. So he went to her, took her hand and helped her up. The fever left her and she began to wait on them.'

— Mark 1:30,31 NIV

When human agency is powerless, the best thing we can do is tell the Lord about it.

DEPENDENCE

'CONSIDER HOW THE WILD FLOWERS GROW ... IF THAT IS HOW GOD CLOTHES THE GRASS OF THE FIELD, ... HOW MUCH MORE WILL HE CLOTHE YOU— YOU OF LITTLE FAITH!'

— LUKE 12:27,28 NIV

The beauty of a wild flower is unmatched, even by royal splendour. Even the lilies of the field remind us that we have a God who cares deeply about our welfare. In every department of life, He makes abundant provision.

'COME TO ME, ALL YOU WHO LABOUR AND ARE HEAVY LADEN, AND I WILL GIVE YOU REST.'

— MAT. 11:27 NKJV

The cares of the school of life are a massive burden. Hand them over to Him and in exchange, He'll give you the easy burden of learning in God's school. *'take my yoke upon you and learn from me, for I am gentle and lowly in heart, and you will find rest for your souls.'* (Mat. 11:27 NKJV)

Deliverance from Depression

'My soul is cast down within me; therefore I remember you from the land of Jordan and of Hermon, from Mount Mizar.'

— Psa 42:6 ESV

David knew that the way out of depression was to remember the God who loved him. Today, we remember that Jesus came from heaven's glory where, like snow-capped Hermon, *'Holiness shines bright'*, down to Mount Calvary. David took his depression to God in prayer. That's the best remedy for us too:

> *'when Satan tempts me to despair...*
> *Upward I look and see Him there,*
> *Who made an end of all my sin.'*

DEVOTION

'JESUS CAME FROM NAZARETH IN GALILEE AND WAS BAPTIZED BY JOHN IN THE JORDAN.'

— MARK 1:9 NIV

For His disciples, baptism symbolised death to the old, sinful nature—and resurrection: the beginning of a new life of faith, empowered by the Spirit of God. For the Lord Jesus Christ, baptism foreshadowed His atoning death for sinners and victorious resurrection in *'the power of an endless life'* (Heb. 7:16). From the outset of His public ministry, He was dedicated to the fulfilment of the divine plan for our salvation—Praise God!

'She did what she could. She poured perfume on my body beforehand to prepare for my burial.'

— Mark 14:8 NIV

They could measure the monetary value of the ointment. But the value of the LORD's Anointed One can never be measured. This woman had a true estimate of His worth - she brought the most valuable thing she had and poured it out on Him— yet, as she well knew, the treasures of this world are,

> *Too mean to speak his worth,*
> *Too mean to set our Saviour forth'.*

— C.H. Hurditch 1839-1908
PHSS 365.

~

'Did you not know that I must be in my Father's house?'

— Luke 2:49 ESV

After three exhausting days, searching every nook and cranny in Jerusalem, Mary and Joseph found Him in the Temple courts, in deep dialogue with experts in the law of Moses. His Father's House held a magnetic attraction for the Son of the Most High. It ought to have been the first place they thought to look for Him.

~

DEVOTION

'WHEN THEY HAD FINISHED BREAKFAST, JESUS SAID TO SIMON PETER, 'SIMON, SON OF JOHN, DO YOU LOVE ME MORE THAN THESE?''

— JOHN 21:15 ESV

The Lord waited till Peter had eaten before dealing with the unresolved question of Peter's devotion. Peter had boasted of greater love than the other disciples, then denied knowing Him. This had to be addressed. How directly, yet sensitively, the Lord spoke to Peter and repaired the damage.

Difficulty

'THE MEN WERE TALKING OF STONING HIM ... BUT DAVID FOUND STRENGTH IN THE LORD HIS GOD. THEN DAVID SAID TO ABIATHAR THE PRIEST, THE SON OF AHIMELEK, 'BRING ME THE EPHOD."

— 1 SAM. 30:6,7 NIV

The secret of David's success was this: he sought the LORD's guidance in all that he did. His behaviour was governed by the word of God. When he came up against challenging circumstances and didn't know what to do, he asked the LORD for direction.

Divine Guidance and Direction

'After the wind there was an earthquake, but the Lord was not in the earthquake. After the earthquake came a fire, but the Lord was not in the fire. And after the fire came a gentle whisper...Then a voice said to him, 'What are you doing here, Elijah?"

— 1 Kings 19:11-13 NIV

Sometimes we mistake noise and activity for the voice of God. But if he is not in it, it's wasted energy. We need to hear the voice of God, the sound of gentle stillness, the still small voice of the Holy Spirit who whispers *'this is the way, walk ye in it'*. (Isaiah 30:21 RV)

'...As long as he sought the Lord, God gave him success.'

— 2 Chron. 26:5 NIV

This is the secret of success in life:

'...do not worry, saying, 'What shall we eat?' or 'What shall we drink?' or 'What shall we wear?'... But seek first his kingdom and his righteousness, and all these things will be given to you as well.'

— Matthew 6:31,33 NIV

∼

The Lord will guide you always; he will satisfy your needs...

— Isaiah 58:11 NIV

This promise is made to those who fulfil the conditions of the preceding two verses:

'if you do away with the yoke of oppression, the pointing finger and malicious talk, and...spend yourselves in behalf of the hungry and satisfy the needs of the oppressed...' (Isaiah 58:9,10)

> *'It is the way the Master went,*
> *Should not the servant tread it still?'*

— H. Bonar

Divine Guidance and Direction

The Lamb at the centre of the throne will be their shepherd; 'he will lead them to springs of living water.

— Rev. 7:17

Let the one who walks in the dark, who has no light, trust in the name of the Lord and rely on their God.

— Isaiah 50:10 NIV

What a comfort to know that when dark times come, as they surely will, I can rely completely on God to help me. If I place my hand in His with childlike faith, He will guide me safely around every obstacle; He will lead me through the darkness of life's conundrums, into the perfect light and warmth of His presence and His love.

Joseph ...had in mind to divorce her quietly. But ...an angel of the Lord appeared to him in a dream and said, '...what is conceived in her is from the Holy Spirit...to fulfill what the Lord had said through the prophet: 'The virgin will conceive and give birth to a son, and they will call him Immanuel (which means 'God with us').

— Matt 1:19-23 NIV

Joseph's crisis of conscience was only resolved when the angel revealed that Mary was God's chosen vessel to fulfil this ancient prophecy. The word of God gave him the confidence and courage to take Mary to be his wife.

He tends his flock like a shepherd: He gathers the lambs in his arms and carries them close to his heart; he gently leads those that have young.

— Isaiah 40:11 NIV

'I have a Shepherd, One I love so well,
How He has blessed me tongue can never tell;
On the cross He suffered, shed His blood and died,
That I might ever in His love confide.' (L. Weaver, 1894)

Divine Judgement

For the word of God is alive and active. Sharper than any double-edged sword, it penetrates even to dividing soul and spirit, joints and marrow; it judges the thoughts and attitudes of the heart.

— Heb 4:12 NIV

God is the great divider: He divided between darkness and light; water and dry land; fish and fowl, animal and humankind. He weighs and divides our thoughts and actions, He divides between good and evil. Nothing escapes His notice! *'He sees, He hears, He knows.'* His judgements are perfect.

A BIBLE VERSE EACH DAY

God's patience waited in the days of Noah, while the ark was being prepared...

— 1 Peter 3:20 ESV

To a violent, immoral world, Noah proclaimed righteousness and reverence for God. Was God in a hurry to judge? No, *'the long-suffering of God waited...'* In today's increasingly violent and immoral world, we continue to hold out God's message of grace:

'whoever hears my word and believes him who sent me has eternal life. He does not come into judgment, but has passed from death to life.' (John 5:24)

Divine light

And God said, 'Let there be light,' and there was light.

— Gen. 1:3 NIV)

God spoke light into being before he created sun or moon. John wrote, *'God is light'* (1 John 1:5 NIV). Isaiah wrote, *'Let the one who walks in the dark, who has no light, trust in the name of the LORD and rely on their God'* (Is. 50:8 NIV). Jesus said, *'I am the light of the world. Whoever follows me will never walk in darkness, but will have the light of life'* (John 8:12 NIV).

If you want light, follow Him.

A BIBLE VERSE EACH DAY

Your word is a lamp for my feet, a light on my path.

— Ps 119:105 NIV

I have come into the world as a light, so that no one who believes in me should stay in darkness.

— John 12:35,46

Jesus, the Living Word of God, shone the light of Divine truth into our spiritual and moral darkness. Faith in Him alone dispels the darkness; His Word shows us how to live on our journey home to heaven.

The opening of your words gives light

— Ps 119:130, RV

As a doorway opens and unfolds things that were previously unseen and unknown to the mind, so the Word of God is like the opening of a door, an entrance into the realms of the Divine: the Word of God sheds the light of Divine Truth in our hearts and reveals the hidden treasures of the knowledge of God and His Love, to our souls.

Divine light

> Unity...like precious oil...as if the dew of Hermon were falling on Mount Zion
>
> — Psalm 133:1-3 NIV

The morning dew is pure, refreshing and life giving. It signals the dawn, the rising of the sun, the light of a new day. On the day He was born, Jesus gave rise to the light of an eternal day; out of the darkness of Calvary, He brought hope to fallen man, the light of Divine Love, forgiveness and peace, the sure hope of eternal life through faith in His ever-precious Name.

> In him was life, and the life was the light of men. The light shines in the darkness, and the darkness has not overcome it.
>
> — John 1:4,5 ESV

Spiritual darkness and moral darkness are dispelled by 'the Word', this divine person who is the source of eternal light and life. He 'shines in the darkness'. He overcomes darkness and evil; He lights up forever the lives of all who put their trust in Him.

A BIBLE VERSE EACH DAY

The true light that gives light to everyone was coming into the world.

— John 1:9 NIV

The sense of the Greek word translated 'true' here, is *'not true as opposed to false, but true in the sense of ideal perfection'.* (Ellicott). It's the difference between the light of a candle compared to the brightness of the noonday sun. John the Baptist's preaching was like candlelight compared to that of the Lord Jesus, who shone with the full strength of original, uncreated light, light that has no equal.

I have come into the world as a light, so that no one who believes in me should stay in darkness.

— John 12:35,46 NIV

Jesus, the Living Word of God, shone the light of Divine truth into our spiritual and moral darkness. Faith in Him alone dispels the darkness; His Word shows us how to live on our journey home to heaven.

Divine Perspective and Divine Power

THERE IS A GOD IN HEAVEN WHO REVEALS SECRETS, AND HE HAS SHOWN KING NEBUCHADNEZZAR WHAT WILL HAPPEN IN THE FUTURE.

— DAN. 2:28 NLT

God, who knows the end from the beginning, revealed many things to Daniel which are yet to be fulfilled. Nebuchadnezzar's dream and further visions given to Daniel and the Apostle John on the Isle of Patmos, revealed that when the empires of this world have had their day, *'the Anointed one'* (Dan. 9:26), the *'KING OF KINGS AND LORD OF LORDS'* (Rev.19:16)—will rule over the kingdom of God forever.

King Hezekiah and the prophet Isaiah son of Amoz cried out in prayer to heaven about this. And the Lord sent an angel, who annihilated all the fighting men and the commanders and officers in the camp of the Assyrian king. So he withdrew to his own land in disgrace.

— 2 Chron 32:20,21 NIV

God is still on the throne. All the power of heaven is available to His servants in time of need, therefore we need not fear the threats of mere men.

'Prayer moves the arm that moves the world.' (Spurgeon)

He spreads out the northern skies over empty space, He suspends the earth over nothing.

— Job 26:7 NIV)

What huge, invisible forces hold the earth in it's controlled orbit of the sun. Men of science estimate earth's weight in TRILLIONS of tons - God hangs it in EMPTY SPACE! Yet, when we think that the One through whom the worlds were made' who was 'wrapped in swaddling bands' by a mother's tender hands - was hanged on a cross for us: we acknowledge that creation is only a whisper of His Redeeming Love and Grace.

Divine Perspective and Divine Power

> Was my arm too short to deliver you? Do I lack the strength to rescue you?
>
> — Isaiah 50:2 NIV

The answers to the LORD's rhetorical questions is obvious. His ability to redeem Israel was not diminished. His power to save was still the same. When things seem to be against us, instead of looking around in dismay we should look up and renew our trust in the unchanging power and love of God, our Rock and our Redeemer.

> 'Lord, save me.' Jesus immediately reached out his hand and took hold of him.
>
> — Matt 14:30,31 ESV

The Lord Jesus is always willing to respond to a cry for help. When a man or a woman recognises their own inability to save themselves and cries out for Divine mercy, the hand of the Saviour is immediately extended in saving power.

'STRETCH OUT YOUR HAND.' HE STRETCHED IT OUT, AND HIS HAND WAS COMPLETELY RESTORED. THEN THE PHARISEES WENT OUT AND BEGAN TO PLOT WITH THE HERODIANS HOW THEY MIGHT KILL JESUS.

— MARK 3:5,6 NIV

Never before had anyone regenerated and restored muscle, bone and sinew to full working order. The Lord Jesus did it instantly, with four words. No post-operative physio required! In the face of such divine power, the blind hatred of the Pharisees was inexcusable. They should have welcomed their Messiah and glorified God!

YET I WILL LEAVE SEVEN THOUSAND IN ISRAEL, ALL THE KNEES THAT HAVE NOT BOWED TO BAAL...

— 1 KINGS 19:18 ESV

Elijah learned that his own imperfect knowledge of the situation was not the sum total of all there was to know about it. Elijah learned that God had 7000 more arrows in his quiver; faithful men who were waiting on their Lord to send help from on High.

Divine Perspective and Divine Power

Giving joyful thanks to the Father, who has...brought us into the kingdom of the Son he loves, in whom we have redemption, the forgiveness of sins. The Son is the image of the invisible God, the firstborn over all creation. For in him all things were created: things in heaven and on earth, visible and invisible, whether thrones or powers or rulers or authorities; all things have been created through him and for him. He is before all things, and in him all things hold together.

— Col 1:12-17 NIV

ll things, including ourselves, owe their existence and allegiance to this Supreme, Eternal Person.

The second beast was given power to give breath to the image of the first beast...

— Rev 13:15 NIV

He is '*given* power' to create a breathing, functioning clone of the Anti-Christ - a masterpiece of Satanic deception. However, 'the lights will be on, but there will be nobody home'. By contrast, Adam was made in the image of God, with an indestructible spiritual dimension to his existence: *'man became a living soul.'* (Gen 2:7) Only God has power to give life that crosses from time into eternity.

HE UPHOLDS THE UNIVERSE BY THE WORD OF HIS POWER...

IN HIM ALL THINGS HOLD TOGETHER.

— HEB 1:3 ESV, COL 1:17 ESV

With 'the word of his power' the Lord Jesus stilled the raging sea, restored sight to the blind, made the deaf to hear; cleansed the lepers, raised the dead. But when it came to Calvary's cross, He was silent. *'Himself He could not save, Love's stream too deeply flowed, In love Himself He gave To pay the debt we owed...'* (A.Midlane, PHSS no. 17). The power of Divine love is truly supernatural and surpasses all the miracles combined!

HE WAS SITTING AND LISTENING AS PAUL PREACHED. LOOKING STRAIGHT AT HIM, PAUL REALIZED HE HAD FAITH TO BE HEALED. SO PAUL CALLED TO HIM IN A LOUD VOICE, 'STAND UP!' AND THE MAN JUMPED TO HIS FEET AND STARTED WALKING.

— ACTS 14:8-10 NLT

He was a paraplegic from birth. Convinced by Paul's preaching, he believed God could heal him. Paul, who had absolute faith in the power of the living God, was the conduit through which God accomplished this miracle. *'Thy power and grace are still the same, Let endless praise exalt Thy name.'* (Isaac Watts 1674-1748 PHSS 113)

Divine Protection and Divine Care

No weapon formed against you will succeed, and you will refute any accusation raised against you in court. This is the heritage of the LORD's servants, and their righteousness is from Me.

— Isaiah 54:17 HCSB)

Those who love the Word of God and faithfully put it into practice in their lives, are assured of His protection from those who would try to harm them or falsely accuse them of wrongdoing.

> Then you will know that I am the Lord, when I bring you into the land of Israel, the land I had sworn with uplifted hand to give to your ancestors.
>
> — Ezekiel 20:42 NIV

In 1947 Israel became a nation again. After nearly 2000 years, God brought them back to the land He promised them. There, He is going to refine them in the fire of tribulation and they will return to Him in their hearts. What God starts, He finishes!

∼

> The Lord is good, a refuge in times of trouble. He cares for those who trust in him.
>
> — Nahum 1:7 NIV

The essential nature of our all-powerful Creator is goodness and love, of a quality far beyond the love and care we have for each other. Time and again those who trust Him have proved how much God cares for their spiritual, mental and physical wellbeing. His love is a well that never runs dry.

∼

Divine Protection and Divine Care

THIS IS WHAT THE LORD ALMIGHTY SAYS ... WHOEVER TOUCHES YOU TOUCHES THE APPLE OF HIS EYE.

— Zechariah 2:8 NIV

Israel has a special place in God's heart. So also do His New Covenant people in the House of God, which is 'pillar and ground of the truth.' Individually and collectively, those who are faithful to Him in every era, are assured of His protection and His presence with them.

Look at the birds of the air; they do not sow or reap or store away in barns, and yet your heavenly Father feeds them. Are you not much more valuable than they?

— Matt 6:26 NIV

Said the Robin to the Sparrow:
'I should really like to know
Why these anxious human beings
Rush about and worry so.'
Said the Sparrow to the Robin:
'Friend, I think that it must be
That they have no Heavenly Father
Such as cares for you and me.'

— E. Cheney, 1859

Are not two sparrows sold for a penny? And not one of them will fall to the ground apart from your Father. But even the hairs of your head are all numbered. Fear not, therefore; you are of more value than many sparrows.

— Mat. 10:29-31 ESV

Disciples of Christ are so highly valued by the Lord that he knows how many individual hairs we have on our heads. *'whoever touches you touches the apple of his eye.'* (Zecheriah 2:8 NIV)

∽

A bruised reed he will not break, and a smouldering wick he will not snuff out...In his name the nations will put their hope.

— Matt 12:20,21 NIV

The Lord Jesus didn't callously sweep aside the needs those who were bruised by the vicissitudes of life, or stamp out the dimly burning light of those who *'followed afar off'*. He tended and nurtured people like Matthew the publican, whose vision was clouded with the things of this world - until *'Jesus, the Sun,'* His *'night broke through and gave [him] light divine'.* (PHSS 85)

∽

ELECTION, FREEWILL AND SOVEREIGN GRACE

THEY CRIED OUT, 'LORD, HAVE MERCY ON US' ...
JESUS CALLED THEM...IN PITY TOUCHED THEIR EYES,
AND IMMEDIATELY THEY RECOVERED THEIR SIGHT

— MATT 20:30-34 ESV

They called on Jesus - then HE called them. Here we see both Divine election and man's freewill in operation. Two blind men were ready to receive Christ, therefore Christ was ready to receive them. They erected no barriers of human pride or self-righteousness to prevent His work of Grace - they opened their hearts and their souls and their lives were flooded with the Light of God's Love!

FOR GOD DID PUT IN THEIR HEARTS TO DO HIS MIND, AND TO COME TO ONE MIND, AND TO GIVE THEIR KINGDOM UNTO THE BEAST, UNTIL THE WORDS OF GOD SHOULD BE ACCOMPLISHED.

— REV. 17;17 RV

These godless leaders of the nations will think they are acting independently, when all the time, they are carrying out the idea that God has put into their hearts. Even when his enemies appear to be gaining the upper hand, He is in complete control. He is working out his sovereign will even through those who hate Him.

NO ONE CAN COME TO ME UNLESS THE FATHER WHO SENT ME DRAWS THEM, AND I WILL RAISE THEM UP AT THE LAST DAY.

— JOHN 6:44 NIV

The impulse to seek after God comes from God. This is true for both saint and sinner: *'Behold I stand at the door and knock'* was the message given to backsliding believers in the Church of God in Laodicea. If Jesus is knocking on the door of your heart today, will you let Him in or shut Him out?

Election, Freewill and Sovereign Grace

> Then the LORD said to Moses, 'Go in to Pharaoh and say to him, 'Thus says the LORD, the God of the Hebrews, 'Let my people go, that they may serve me.
>
> — Exodus 9:1 ESV

If the LORD had not come down to deliver His people, they would never have escaped from slavery. If the Lord Jesus had not come down from heaven we could never have eternal redemption. As the old hymn says:

> *'Who is a pardoning God like Thee?*
> *Or who has grace, so rich and free?'*
>
> — S. Davies 1723-1761,
> PHSS 112

Encouragement

ARISE AND BE DOING, AND THE LORD BE WITH THEE.

— 1 CHRONICLES 22:16 RV

David's words to Solomon, as he charged him to build a house for Jehovah, are full of energy and encouragement. These words still resonate with all who are engaged in building God's spiritual house today.

Go and enjoy choice food and sweet drinks, and send some to those who have nothing prepared. This day is holy to our Lord. Do not grieve, for the joy of the Lord is your strength.

— Nehemiah 8:10 NIV

When the law of Moses was read and clearly explained, the remnant of Israel wept for their failure to keep it. However, their leaders exhorted them to rejoice: the Word of God, exalted in their hearts, led to willing, united obedience and resulted in great spiritual enrichment and blessing.

'You are my servant'; I have chosen you and have not rejected you. So do not fear, for I am with you; do not be dismayed, for I am your God. I will strengthen you and help you; I will uphold you with my righteous right hand.

— Isaiah 41:9,10 NIV

Those who are called to serve God can be sure of His help, no matter how great the challenges they face.

'Wherever He leads thee, go, valiantly go,
And stand, like the brave, with thy face to the
foe.'

— Anon, PHSS 392

The End of This Present World

THE HEAVENS WILL VANISH LIKE SMOKE, THE EARTH WILL WEAR OUT LIKE A GARMENT... BUT MY SALVATION WILL LAST FOREVER, MY RIGHTEOUSNESS WILL NEVER FAIL.' (ISAIAH 51:6 NIV) 'THE DAY OF GOD ... WILL BRING ABOUT THE DESTRUCTION OF THE HEAVENS BY FIRE, AND THE ELEMENTS WILL MELT IN THE HEAT. BUT IN KEEPING WITH HIS PROMISE WE ARE LOOKING FORWARD TO A NEW HEAVEN AND A NEW EARTH, WHERE RIGHTEOUSNESS DWELLS.

— 2 PETER 3:12,13 NIV

Peter repeats what God previously revealed to Isaiah about the ultimate end of this present world and the eternal security of those who trust in the salvation God has provided.

Heaven and earth will pass away, but my words will never pass away. 'But about that day or hour no one knows, not even the angels in heaven, nor the Son, but only the Father.

— Matthew 24:35,36 NIV

This present world and the universe in which it exists will be replaced by a new heaven and a new earth, perfect and untainted by sin (2 Pet. 3:12). It is no secret that the Lord Jesus will return to earth at the end of the tribulation period. However, the day and hour of the dissolving of heaven and earth is known only to the Father. Only God the Father knows when the heavens and the earth He created will be burned up (see Is. 34:4; 2 Pet. 3:12). The day shall declare it.

Heaven and earth will pass away, but my words will not pass away. But concerning that day or that hour, no one knows, not even the angels in heaven, nor the Son, but only the Father.

— Mark 13:31,32 ESV

Eternal View

Boaz replied, 'I've been told all about what you have done for your mother-in-law since the death of your husband -how you left your father and mother and your homeland and came to live with a people you did not know before'.

— Ruth 2:11 NIV

Boaz knew all about Ruth before she came to glean in his fields. However, he did not know at this point what lay in store for them both! In the Lord Jesus Christ, we have a kinsman-redeemer who not only knows all about us but also knows what a wonderful eternal future lies ahead for all who put their trust in Him.

HE SHALL SEE HIS SEED...HE SHALL SEE OF THE TRAVAIL OF HIS SOUL, AND SHALL BE SATISFIED

— ISAIAH 53:10,11 KJV

The central purpose of God's grace is to redeem a people that are the seed, the 'offspring' of the atoning death of His Son on Calvary's cross where his soul was made 'an offering for sin'. And because of His victorious death and resurrection, the day is now fixed with absolute certainty, when He will be fully satisfied with the results of His suffering.

THE SONS OF THIS WORLD ARE MORE SHREWD IN DEALING WITH THEIR OWN GENERATION THAN THE SONS OF LIGHT.

— LUKE 16:8 ESV

The worldly person invests everything in getting on and making their mark in this life because that's all they have; whereas the person who has the light of eternal life in their heart can afford to see things from an eternal perspective.

Eternal view

WHOEVER HEARS MY WORD AND BELIEVES HIM WHO SENT ME HAS ETERNAL LIFE AND WILL NOT BE JUDGED BUT HAS CROSSED OVER FROM DEATH TO LIFE.

— JOHN 5:24 NIV)

The words of the Lord Jesus Christ give hope for tomorrow. He enables those who believe on Him to rise above and see beyond their present uncertainties and difficulties. Eternal peace and prosperity belong to those who take Him at His word. What a wonderful Saviour!

YOU HAVE SORROW NOW, BUT I WILL SEE YOU AGAIN, AND YOUR HEARTS WILL REJOICE, AND NO ONE WILL TAKE YOUR JOY FROM YOU...IN THE WORLD YOU WILL HAVE TRIBULATION. BUT TAKE HEART; I HAVE OVERCOME THE WORLD.

— JOHN 16:22,33 ESV

The Lord Jesus prepared His disciples beforehand for His death and resurrection. He gave them a sure hope, something to hold on to when all seemed lost, when His enemies appeared to have the upper hand. The promise of His return and the joy that flows from His triumphant resurrection, no-one can ever take away.

THE TRUMPET WILL SOUND, THE DEAD WILL BE RAISED IMPERISHABLE, AND WE WILL BE CHANGED. FOR THE PERISHABLE MUST CLOTHE ITSELF WITH THE IMPERISHABLE, AND THE MORTAL WITH IMMORTALITY.

— 1 Corinthians 15:52,53 NIV

There will be a succession of trumpet blasts, alerting us that the moment we've been waiting for, has come. As the final trumpet sounds, we will be rid of these old perishable bodies and will be clothed with new, imperishable, immortal bodies which can never sin and will never die! What a memorable day that will be!

IN HOPE OF ETERNAL LIFE, WHICH GOD, WHO CANNOT LIE, PROMISED BEFORE TIMES ETERNAL.

— Titus 1:2 R.V.

God cannot lie. In the dateless past, God promised eternal life. The Lord Jesus Christ came to make good that promise. He said 'whoever hears my word and believes him who sent me has eternal life' and *'everyone who lives and believes in me shall never die'* (John 5:24; 11:26 ESV). God always keeps His promises.

> THE HEAVENS WILL VANISH LIKE SMOKE, THE EARTH WILL WEAR OUT LIKE A GARMENT... BUT MY SALVATION WILL LAST FOREVER, MY RIGHTEOUSNESS WILL NEVER FAIL.
>
> — ISAIAH 51:6 NIV

> THE DAY OF GOD ... WILL BRING ABOUT THE DESTRUCTION OF THE HEAVENS BY FIRE, AND THE ELEMENTS WILL MELT IN THE HEAT. BUT IN KEEPING WITH HIS PROMISE WE ARE LOOKING FORWARD TO A NEW HEAVEN AND A NEW EARTH, WHERE RIGHTEOUSNESS DWELLS.
>
> — 2 PETER 3:12,13 NIV

Peter repeats what God previously revealed to Isaiah about the ultimate end of this present world and the eternal security of those who trust in the salvation God has provided.

EVIL

EVEN THOUGH SOMEONE IS PURSUING YOU TO TAKE YOUR LIFE, THE LIFE OF MY LORD WILL BE BOUND SECURELY IN THE BUNDLE OF THE LIVING BY THE LORD YOUR GOD...WHEN THE LORD HAS FULFILLED FOR MY LORD EVERY GOOD THING HE PROMISED ...

— 1 SAMUEL 25:29,30 NIV

All who suffer with Christ will know His presence and His help. They also have the promise of future glory: *'Faithful is the saying: For if we died with him, we shall also live with him: if we endure, we shall also reign with him'* (2 Tim. 2:11,12).

A BIBLE VERSE EACH DAY

> YOUR EYES ARE TOO PURE TO LOOK ON EVIL; YOU CANNOT TOLERATE WRONGDOING. WHY THEN DO YOU TOLERATE THE TREACHEROUS? WHY ARE YOU SILENT WHILE THE WICKED SWALLOW UP THOSE MORE RIGHTEOUS THAN THEMSELVES?
>
> — HABAKKUK 1:13 NIV

It's not wrong to ask God why He lets bad things happen. Habakkuk couldn't make sense of it until he took it to the Lord in prayer. God's answer was unequivocal: divine deliverance from oppressive evil will come and faithfulness to Him will pay off in the end. Faith shines brightest in the dark.

～

> AN ANGEL...SEIZED THE DRAGON, THAT ANCIENT SERPENT...AND BOUND HIM FOR A THOUSAND YEARS...AFTER THAT, HE MUST BE SET FREE FOR A SHORT TIME.
>
> — REVELATION 20:1-3 NIV

The natural mind asks 'Why does God not deal with Satan once and for all? Why allow him to introduce his deadly poison yet again?' God answers: *'as the heavens are higher than the earth, so are my ways higher than your ways, and my thoughts than your thoughts.'* (Is. 55:9).

> *'God is His own Interpreter,*
> *And He will make it plain.'*
> (William Cowper PHSS 176)

Excuses

'Lord, first let me go and bury my father.' Jesus said to him, 'Let the dead bury their own dead, but you go and proclaim the kingdom of God.'

— Luke 9:59,60 NIV

The Lord Jesus didn't object to the man paying his last respects to his father. He rebuked the man for using the death of his father as an excuse for not following Him. As a committed follower of Christ, the man could have gone to his father's funeral and proclaimed the glorious hope of the kingdom of God!

The Exaltation of Christ

He who descended is the very one who ascended higher than all the heavens, in order to fill the whole universe.

— Ephesians 4:10 NIV

'A universe without Christ ascended and glorified would be as the world without the sun. He shall fill all things with His presence; His fulness, His blessing and His glory will give a new and full meaning to creation' (John Miller).

Eyewitnesses of His Majesty

WE HAVE SEEN HIS GLORY, THE GLORY OF THE ONE AND ONLY SON, WHO CAME FROM THE FATHER, FULL OF GRACE AND TRUTH.

— JOHN 1:14 NIV

Even though John, Peter and James were privileged to see Him transfigured *'in the holy mount'* - (holy because Jesus was there) - which was truly glorious to behold; they also heard His gracious yet gripping words and saw the awesome glory of His miraculous deeds of kindness, which in themselves bore witness to His divine nature.

Falling Short

THEY WORSHIPPED THE LORD, BUT THEY ALSO SERVED THEIR OWN GODS.

— 2 KINGS 17:33 NIV

How often has this error been repeated! Modes of worship that are diametrically opposed to the Word of God are introduced alongside the pure, Bible-based, worship of God.

Beliefs and practices that are alien to the Word of God have no place among His people.

A BIBLE VERSE EACH DAY

HE WAS GREATLY HELPED UNTIL HE BECAME POWERFUL. BUT AFTER UZZIAH BECAME POWERFUL, HIS PRIDE LED TO HIS DOWNFALL. HE WAS UNFAITHFUL TO THE LORD HIS GOD.

— 2 CHRON 26:15,16 NIV

He started well but finished badly. Full of his own importance, King Uzziah thought he had the right to do as he pleased in the sanctuary of God. Sudden and swift judgement followed. *'let him that thinketh he standeth take heed lest he fall'* (1 Cor. 10:12 R.V.)

I LOOKED FOR SOMEONE AMONG THEM WHO WOULD BUILD UP THE WALL AND STAND BEFORE ME IN THE GAP ON BEHALF OF THE LAND SO I WOULD NOT HAVE TO DESTROY IT, BUT I FOUND NO ONE.

— EZEKIEL 22:30 NIV

God is looking for faithful servants, who will stand up for what is right and true according to His Word. He expects those who have known His mercy to point others to the Saviour of sinners. Don't let Him down.

Falling Short

AND AGAIN HE CAME AND FOUND THEM SLEEPING, FOR THEIR EYES WERE HEAVY.

— MATT 26:43 ESV

At the very moment when His whole being wrestled in prayer with God, Peter, James and John failed to give Him the little moral support He asked from them. How alone He was! Thank God — human failings could never deflect the Lord Jesus from the great redemptive purpose for which He had come. But it cost Him more than we will ever know to say: 'your will be done'.

WE MUST PAY THE MOST CAREFUL ATTENTION, THEREFORE, TO WHAT WE HAVE HEARD, SO THAT WE DO NOT DRIFT AWAY. FOR SINCE THE MESSAGE SPOKEN THROUGH ANGELS WAS BINDING, AND EVERY VIOLATION AND DISOBEDIENCE RECEIVED ITS JUST PUNISHMENT, HOW SHALL WE ESCAPE IF WE IGNORE SO GREAT A SALVATION?

— HEBREWS 2:1-3 NIV

If the Lord Jesus does not have the first place in our hearts, we will drift towards self-choosing and self-pleasing. We need to cultivate His presence, by reading, prayer, and meditation on His word. Disobedience and neglect will bring punishment instead of blessing, and loss of eternal reward.

Personal Faith

That night the Lord appeared to him and said, '...Do not be afraid, for I am with you...' Isaac built an altar there [*Beersheba*] and called on the name of the Lord. There he pitched his tent.

— Genesis 26:23-25 NIV

The building of an altar, a place of worship, was an act of faith. Isaac pitched his tent in the place where God revealed Himself. He knew his prosperity came from God.

> *'And every virtue we possess,*
> *And every victory won,*
> *And every thought of holiness,*
> *Are His alone.'*
>
> — H. Auber 1773-1862

A BIBLE VERSE EACH DAY

Isaac reopened the wells that had been dug in the time of his father Abraham, which the Philistines had stopped up after Abraham died, and he gave them the same names his father had given them.

— Gen 26:18 NIV

The Philistines filled in the wells with earth. They 'rubbished' the claims that faith had made. Isaac re-dug the wells and called them by the same names that his father Abraham had called them. Re-staking his claim to the inheritance God had promised was an act of faith.

~

Jacob called the name of the place Peniel, saying, 'For I have seen God face to face, and yet my life has been delivered'.

— Genesis 32:31 ESV

After Peniel, Jacob was weaker yet stronger than before. Each step reminded him of his human weakness but also reminded him that God had touched him, that God's hand was on the tiller of his life.

> *One step thou seest - then go forward boldly,*
> *One step is far enough for faith to see;*
> *Take that, and thy next duty shall be told thee,*
> *For STEP BY STEP thy Lord is leading thee.*

— Anonymous

Personal Faith

The Lord said to Moses, 'Why do you cry to me? Tell the people of Israel to go forward.'

— Exodus 14:15 ESV

Sometimes it is necessary to *'... halt (no track discovering), Fearful lest we go astray...'* At such times it is wise to wait on the Lord in prayer. But when the clear direction of God comes, we must step out in faith, *'being fully persuaded that what he has promised he is able also to do...' (Rom 4:21 Derby).* Today the clear word of the Lord is: 'GO FORWARD!'

∽

And when the Israelites saw the mighty hand of the Lord displayed against the Egyptians, the people feared the Lord and put their trust in him and in Moses his servant.

— Exodus 14:31 NIV

Faith is strengthened by exercise: Israel had to step out in faith, and walk down into the river bed. Only when they reached the other side could they look back and see what God had done for them. The individual, personal exercise of faith strengthened their trust in God and in Moses' divinely inspired leadership.

∽

MAY YOUR FAMILY BE LIKE THAT OF PEREZ, WHOM TAMAR BORE TO JUDAH...AND SHE GAVE BIRTH TO A SON...HE WAS THE FATHER OF JESSE, THE FATHER OF DAVID.

— RUTH 4:12,13,17 NIV

There is Gentile blood in the royal line of the kings of Judah. The royal line which continued on through David culminated in the Son of David who was born in Bethlehem and shed His precious blood for us on the cross: Jesus the Son of God the redeemer of both Jew and Gentile. Can you say: ' He is MY redeemer?

AND THE PEOPLE OF JUDAH WERE VICTORIOUS BECAUSE THEY RELIED ON THE LORD, THE GOD OF THEIR ANCESTORS.

— 2 CHRONICLES 13:18 NIV

Am I relying on the LORD or on my own strength? Victory is assured when we lean on The LORD and let Him fight our battles.

'Stand in his strength alone;
The arm of flesh will fail you,
You dare not trust your own.' (G. Duffield)

PERSONAL FAITH

SO HE WILL DO TO ME WHATEVER HE HAS PLANNED. HE CONTROLS MY DESTINY.

— JOB 23:14 NLT

Job believed his life was ordered by God. He viewed the events of his life, not as random accidents but as the outworking of God's purposes for him, even though he couldn't understand why calamity after calamity had overtaken him; even though his friends misunderstood God's purposes and accused Job of bringing it all on himself because of his sins.

'the eyes of the Lord are on those who fear him, on those whose hope is in his unfailing love, to deliver them from death and keep them alive in famine. We wait in hope for the Lord; he is our help and our shield. In him our hearts rejoice, for we trust in his holy name. May your unfailing love be with us, Lord, even as we put our hope in you.' (Psalm 33:18-22 NIV)

IF YOU HAVE FAITH AND DO NOT DOUBT...YOU CAN SAY TO THIS MOUNTAIN, 'GO, THROW YOURSELF INTO THE SEA,' AND IT WILL BE DONE. IF YOU BELIEVE, YOU WILL RECEIVE WHATEVER YOU ASK FOR IN PRAYER.

— MATTHEW 21:21,22 NIV

Does this mean followers of Christ have carte blanche to get anything they want? Far from it. Faith in God is only effective if we ask according to His will:

'if we ask anything according to his will, he hears us.' (1 John 5:14) Misplaced faith and self-centred requests will be ignored.

~

ACCORDING TO YOUR FAITH LET IT BE DONE TO YOU.

— MATTHEW 9:29 NIV

Who is Jesus? A great miracle worker, rejected as king by both Jew and Gentile 2000 years ago? The Bible tells us he was the Son of God. God in human form. One of the Trinity, Father Son and Holy Spirit, yet One God; it baffles human intelligence and can only be received by faith.

> *'Who is he in yonder stall*
> *At whose feet the shepherds fall?*
> *Tis the Lord Oh wondrous story,*
> *Tis the Lord, the king of glory*
> *At his feet we humbly fall,*
> *Laud him own him Lord of all.'*

— B. R. HANBY 1833-1867

Personal Faith

> He said to her, 'Daughter, your faith has healed you. Go in peace and be freed from your suffering.'
>
> — Mark 5:34 NIV

The Lord really meant 'your faith IN ME has made you whole.' If the woman had touched a lamp-post would she have been healed? Of course not. True peace only comes when faith touches the source of divine power.

> By faith in the name of Jesus, this man whom you see and know was made strong. It is Jesus' name and the faith that comes through him that has completely healed him.
>
> — Acts 3:16 NIV

It was not the strength of Peter's faith that healed the lame man. It was the healing power of the life-giving name of Jesus of Nazareth. Peter's confidence was in the One he had seen performing countless miracles during the previous three and a half years. No other name possesses such power.

>WHEN NEITHER SUN NOR STARS APPEARED FOR MANY DAYS AND THE STORM CONTINUED RAGING, WE FINALLY GAVE UP ALL HOPE OF BEING SAVED... 'DO NOT BE AFRAID, PAUL...GOD HAS GRACIOUSLY GIVEN YOU THE LIVES OF ALL WHO SAIL WITH YOU.'
>
> — ACTS 27:20,24 NIV

Paul was in the same boat as the others. His faith in God was tested too. Only when men had exhausted *'the arm of flesh'* did God step in! What a vindication of Paul's faith in God when the angel stood beside him in the darkness with a welcome message of Divine deliverance!

> FAITH COMES FROM HEARING THE MESSAGE, AND THE MESSAGE IS HEARD THROUGH THE WORD ABOUT CHRIST.
>
> — ROMANS 10:17 NIV

As children, we believe what our parents tell us. *'Faith cometh by hearing'* is true of anything we hear and believe; but in relation to divine matters, hearing comes *'by the word of God.'* The Bible sets forth a saving faith, that is, faith that lays hold of the Saviour of sinners, faith in Jesus Christ, the Living Word of God.

Personal Faith

Without faith it is impossible to please God, because anyone who comes to him must believe that he exists and that he rewards those who earnestly seek him.

— Hebrews 11:6 NIV

Do you believe there is a God? A supreme creator? Do you believe God designed this world for our benefit? Look at a piece of fruit; a plum an apple, a banana - just the right size to pick and eat. Is this an accident of evolution? Do you believe God is interested in your welfare? That's the starting point for faith.

If you do not stand firm in your faith, you will not stand at all.

— Isaiah 7:9 NIV

The Lord, who knows the hearts of all men, gave to King Ahaz fair warning of the consequences of unbelief. He invited Ahaz to ask for a sign and receive confirmation of God's readiness to help him. Ahaz refused and suffered loss. If he had been a man of faith, his fears would have been allayed, he would have looked beyond the immediate crisis and gained the victory.

A BIBLE VERSE EACH DAY

But my righteous one will live by faith. And I take no pleasure in the one who shrinks back.

— Hebrews 10:38

'I am a Hebrew and I worship the LORD, the God of heaven, who made the sea and the dry land.' (Jonah 1:9 NIV) Yes, there is only one true God who made this beautiful world and everything in it. He first spoke through the Old Testament writings and the Hebrew prophets; *'but in these last days he has spoken to us by his Son, whom he appointed heir of all things, and through whom also he made the universe.'* (Heb. 1:2 NIV) *'to the only wise God be glory forever through Jesus Christ! Amen.'* (Rom. 16:27 NIV)

Walking by Faith

Isaac planted crops in that land and the same year reaped a hundredfold, because the Lord blessed him.'

— Genesis 26:12 NIV

Isaac was a man of faith like his father. He sowed seed in faith. His hope was in God, the giver and withholder of blessing. God rewarded his faith with a bumper harvest.

> For if you live according to the flesh, you will die; but if by the Spirit you put to death the misdeeds of the body, you will live.
>
> — Romans 8:13 NIV

Believers on Christ now have a choice which was unavailable to them in unbelief. Thank God for this glorious possibility - not only am I justified in the sight of God but if I choose to, I can walk, live, think and behave by the power of the Holy Spirit, in a way that is pleasing to our God and Saviour.

> We should not trust in ourselves but in God who raises the dead, who delivered us from so great a death, and does deliver us; in whom we trust that He will still deliver us.
>
> — 2 Corinthians 1:9-10 NKJV

Some trust in their own strength; some trust in science; some trust the inventions of mankind to stave off the day of death. *'but we will make mention of the name of the LORD our God'* (Psalm 20:7 RV)

For we have become partakers of Christ if we hold the beginning of our confidence steadfast to the end.

— Hebrews 3:14 NKJV

Becoming a 'partaker of Christ' depends on how strongly we continue to hold on to Him throughout life's journey. We cannot enjoy His fellowship unless we cultivate His friendship. And we cannot have His friendship if we prefer the fellowship of the world.

But we are not of those who draw back to perdition, but of those who believe to the saving of the soul.

— Hebrews 10:39 NKJV

'Perdition means utter loss and here it is the loss of the believer's life. No saved person can shrink back and lose eternal salvation… but a saved man may not have a saved life; all his works may be burned up, yet he himself shall be saved so as by fire … How happy to be amongst those who have faith to the saving of the soul (or life)!' (*John Miller*)

A BIBLE VERSE EACH DAY

> BY FAITH ISAAC BLESSED JACOB AND ESAU IN REGARD TO THEIR FUTURE.
>
> — HEBREWS 11:20 NIV

Isaac faithfully followed Abraham's footsteps. Like all of us he made mistakes, and there were occasions when he *'dropped the ball'* and failed to see the spiritual importance of his actions. Yet despite his clouded vision, in the end, he clearly saw that God had transferred the blessing of the firstborn to Jacob.

From Jacob came Judah, from Judah came the Messiah, our Lord Jesus Christ. Even though we may at times falter, or be *'faint yet pursuing'* (Judges 8:4), God in His grace, still uses imperfect men and women of faith to further His purposes.

Faithfulness

Only be very careful...[RV: *take diligent heed*] to serve him with all your heart and with all your soul.

— Joshua 22:5 ESV

Joshua spoke these words to the Reubenites, Gadites & half tribe of Mannasseh when he discharged them from active military service. How important it is that we do not push the Lord and His things into a corner of our lives; we are exhorted to diligently observe the commands of the Lord, to love Him and devote ourselves to His service with heart & soul.

'All this', David said, 'I have in writing as a result of the Lord's hand on me, and he enabled me to understand all the details of the plan'.

— 1 Chronicles 28:19 NIV

Like Moses before him, and the apostles after him, David was given a detailed plan of the House of God for his day and generation. He did not make it up; he received it from God and followed it to the letter. The pattern for God's house today came from the Lord Jesus to the apostles. We are not at liberty to change it. We must follow it faithfully until '*the end of the age*'.

Fear

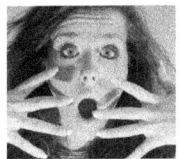

Elijah said to her, 'Don't be afraid.

— 1 Kings 17:13 NIV

Days, perhaps weeks before the widow got down to her last handful of meal, God was at work in the east where he had hidden his servant in the mountains of Jordan. The brook Cherith began to dwindle to a trickle until there was nothing left. And, just when the well seemed to have run dry, God sent Elijah to Zarephath.

'As for God, his way is perfect' (Psalm 18:30 RV)

PREPARE TO MEET YOUR GOD.

— Amos 4:12 NIV

Charles Spurgeon, the great 19th century Baptist preacher, observed that before Adam sinned, he loved to meet God and spend time in His company; also, those who've trusted Jesus as Saviour, love to spend time in His presence and look forward to the day when they will physically meet Him at His return; but for those who live without God, the thought of meeting Him is one of fear and dread.

Jesus told him, 'Don't be afraid; just believe.'

— Mark 5:36 NIV

When all seemed lost, the Lord gave Jairus fresh hope. His faith was not misplaced. Jesus words assured him, all would be well. When we face challenges beyond our control, we must trust the One whose hand is on the tiller of our lives. There is no situation He cannot turn around.

Fruitbearing

POMEGRANATES OF BLUE, PURPLE AND SCARLET YARN AROUND THE HEM OF THE ROBE, WITH GOLD BELLS BETWEEN THEM.

— Exodus 28:33 NIV

Pomegranates represent fruitbearing. There was a rich variety: blue, purple and scarlet.

Blue speaks of the Divine origin of our High Priest; Purple speaks of his Kingship and universal authority; Scarlet speaks of his humility (worm scarlet). As the golden bells sounded between each pomegranate, so in holy and royal priesthood service we must represent and tell out Christ's lovely character.

A BIBLE VERSE EACH DAY

THE PRECIOUS OIL...THAT CAME DOWN UPON THE SKIRT OF HIS GARMENTS UNITY...LIKE PRECIOUS OIL...RUNNING DOWN ON AARON'S BEARD, DOWN ON THE COLLAR OF HIS ROBE.

— PSALM 133:2-3 NIV

Round the hem of Aaron's robes were golden bells and pomegranates of blue, purple, scarlet. (Ex 28:33,34) Pomegranates represent fruitbearing. Blue speaks of the Divine origin and holiness of our High Priest; purple of His supreme authority; scarlet of His humility. In royal priesthood service, with God's help, we can mirror and tell of those characteristics to others.

YOU MAY ASK ME FOR ANYTHING IN MY NAME, AND I WILL DO IT...IF YOU REMAIN IN ME AND MY WORDS REMAIN IN YOU, ASK WHATEVER YOU WISH, AND IT WILL BE DONE FOR YOU... WHATEVER YOU ASK IN MY NAME THE FATHER WILL GIVE YOU.

— JOHN 14:14 & 15:7,16 NIV

The context of these promises is fruit-bearing by disciples who abide in Christ and have His words abiding in them. If they ask in the name of the One who prayed 'not my will but Thine be done' then their requests will be granted and God will be glorified.

Freedom from the Power of Sin

O WRETCHED MAN THAT I AM! WHO WILL DELIVER ME FROM THIS BODY OF DEATH? I THANK GOD— THROUGH JESUS CHRIST OUR LORD!

— ROMANS 7:24-25 NKJV

The only way to be set free from the miserable domination of sin and spiritual death, is by surrendering our fallen nature to Jesus Christ, inviting Him to live in our hearts, and submitting to His authority each day.

A BIBLE VERSE EACH DAY

With freedom did Christ set us free: stand fast therefore, and be not entangled again in a yoke of bondage.

— Galatians 5:1 RV

How easily our old nature can be tempted to turn aside from the glorious freedom Christ has given us! Only by remembering what it cost Him to redeem us, and by crucifying that 'old man', will we continue to live in the fulness of our God-given freedom and avoid a return to the enslavement of sin.

Forgiveness

AFTER JOB HAD PRAYED FOR HIS FRIENDS, THE
LORD RESTORED HIS FORTUNES AND GAVE HIM
TWICE AS MUCH AS HE HAD BEFORE.

— JOB 42:10 NIV

The sequence is important. The very act of praying for those who had 'despitefully used him' enabled Job to forgive, and unlocked the blessing of God. We cannot expect Divine approval or blessing unless we are prepared to forgive: *'Be kind and compassionate to one another, forgiving each other, just as in Christ God forgave you.'* (Ephesians 4:32)

I FORMED YOU; YOU ARE MY SERVANT; O ISRAEL, YOU WILL NOT BE FORGOTTEN BY ME. I HAVE BLOTTED OUT YOUR TRANSGRESSIONS LIKE A CLOUD AND YOUR SINS LIKE MIST; RETURN TO ME, FOR I HAVE REDEEMED YOU.

— ISAIAH 44:21,22 ESV

God speaks to His wayward children with gracious words. They may have forgotten Him but He will never forget them; He makes it easy for them to return because He has already forgiven them. He redeemed them by the blood of a spotless lamb. They owe Him their lives.

REND YOUR HEART, AND NOT YOUR GARMENTS, AND TURN UNTO THE LORD YOUR GOD, FOR HE IS GRACIOUS AND FULL OF COMPASSION, SLOW TO ANGER, AND PLENTEOUS IN MERCY.

— JOEL 3:13 RV

The great Almighty Creator of our souls takes no delight in punitive retribution. He is full of pity for our fallen condition and would far rather show us mercy when we acknowledge our sinful nature and ask His forgiveness: 'everyone who calls on the name of the Lord will be saved' (Joel 2:32 NIV)

Forgiveness

Lord, how many times shall I forgive my brother or sister ... Up to seven times? Jesus answered, I tell you, not seven times, but seventy-seven times.

— Matthew 18:21,22

J esus illustrated this principle by telling the story of a king who forgave a debtor, then sent him to prison because the forgiven debtor refused to forgive a fellow-servant a smaller debt. Jesus said: 'This is how my heavenly Father will treat each of you unless you forgive your brother or sister from your heart.' (v. 35)' If I don't forgive those who ask me for mercy, I will suffer the consequences of God's displeasure.

~

I want you to know that through Jesus the forgiveness of sins is proclaimed to you. Through him everyone who believes is set free from every sin.

— Acts 13:38,39 NIV

'If I come to Jesus,
He will save my soul,
Seal me by His Spirit,
Cleanse, and make me whole.'

— F. Crosby

~

Giving God the First Place in Our Heart

JOTHAM GREW POWERFUL BECAUSE HE WALKED STEADFASTLY BEFORE THE LORD HIS GOD.

— 2 CHRONICLES 27:6 NIV

Other versions translate this as: 'because he ordered his ways...' Jotham, who came to the throne after the death of his father Uzziah, arranged his life in such a way that the things of God had priority. As a result he formed habits of life that resulted in God's blessing. A rock solid foundation which brought great strength and security to his kingdom.

SEEK THE LORD AND LIVE.

— AMOS 5:6 NIV

YOU WILL SEEK ME AND FIND ME WHEN YOU SEEK ME WITH ALL YOUR HEART.

— JEREMIAH 29:13 NIV

When I've lost something very valuable, I go out of my way to find it. God's favour and God's presence are worth far more than anything this world can offer. Shall I seek Him with all my heart today?

THEY BROUGHT THE COIN, AND HE ASKED THEM, 'WHOSE IMAGE IS THIS? AND WHOSE INSCRIPTION?' 'CAESAR'S,' THEY REPLIED. THEN JESUS SAID TO THEM, 'GIVE BACK TO CAESAR WHAT IS CAESAR'S AND TO GOD WHAT IS GOD'S.

— MARK 12:16,17 NIV

It's important to get our work-life balance right. It's even more important to properly divide our resources between God and our employers. Followers of Christ don't shortchange either one. They pay their dues to both.

Giving God the First Place in Our Heart

Mary has chosen what is better, and it will not be taken away from her.

— Luke 10:42 NIV

Mary had her priorities right. We're sure Mary wasn't a lazy person; we believe she just said to herself 'Mary, the dishes can wait; I want to hear what He's saying – because HE is no ordinary person'. The trivialities of the daily round should not take precedence - more important to be nourished by the words of grace that fall from the lips of our Messiah, the Prince of Peace.

With the measure you use, it will be measured to you—and even more. Whoever has will be given more; whoever does not have, even what they have will be taken from them.

— Mark 4:24,25 NIV

The more we give, the more we'll receive, is a universal principle. An old Scots saying says: 'a gauin' fit's aye getting'—meaning: 'an industrious person is always gathering something of value'. The more time and effort you invest in anything, the more you'll get back. The more you open your heart to God, the more God's heart will be opened to you.

> WHOEVER HAS WILL BE GIVEN MORE; WHOEVER DOES NOT HAVE, EVEN WHAT THEY HAVE WILL BE TAKEN FROM THEM.
>
> — MARK 4:25 NIV

The principle enshrined in the Lord's words also works in reverse. Those who devote time and energy to things of no value will be the losers. Those who withhold good from others will experience the same. 'God loves a cheerful giver'—Be generous!

> THERE IS A LAD HERE, WHICH HATH FIVE BARLEY LOAVES, AND TWO FISHES.
>
> — JOHN 6:9 RV

What a generous heart this boy had! He offered his packed lunch to help feed a huge crowd of hungry people. 'but what are these among so many?' said Andrew, who had not yet learned that the LORD, who owns 'the cattle upon a thousand hills' (Ps 50:10), can exponentially multiply what we give to Him for the benefit of others - and we'll still have more left over than we started with!

Giving God the First Place in Our Heart

Here is a boy with five small barley loaves and two small fish ... they...filled twelve baskets with the pieces of the five barley loaves left over...

— John 6:9,13 NIV

The Lord Jesus multiplied a boys willing but insignificant offering, so that it more than met the need of five thousand men, plus women and children! If we but give our hearts to the Saviour of the world, who died and rose again to give us eternal life, He will fill us to overflowing - and then some!

*'...what I can I give Him?
Give my heart.'*

—Christina Rossetti, 1872

Remember this: Whoever sows sparingly will also reap sparingly, and whoever sows generously will also reap generously.

— 2 Corinthians 9:6 NIV

Like the fundamental laws of physics, this is one of God's universal principles. The more we give to Him and to others on His behalf, of our time, our energy, our resources, the more we will be enriched in our own lives. *'whoever loses their life for my sake will find it'* (Matt 10:39).

God's Priorities

THE TEMPLE WAS COMPLETED ON THE THIRD DAY OF THE MONTH ADAR, IN THE SIXTH YEAR OF THE REIGN OF KING DARIUS.

— EZRA 6:15 NIV

This is the date of the recommencement of temple worship in the House of God after 70 years exile in Babylon! A red-letter day! What a wonderful testament to God's faithfulness. He moved Gentile Kings - Cyrus, Darius and Artaxerxes - to promote the repatriation of His people and the restoration of temple worship in His House at Jerusalem! If the house of God was so precious to God then, how much more precious to God is our service in His Spiritual House today?

Good News!

He has sent me to proclaim freedom for the prisoners and recovery of sight for the blind, to set the oppressed free, to proclaim the year of the Lord's favour.

— Luke 4:18,19 NIV

Israel's 'Jubilee' year began on the Day of Atonement in the 49th year because the 50th year was the year when all who were in debt were set free! Jesus came from heaven to set us free: to proclaim God's good news to Jew and Gentile alike:

> 'Sound the trumpet, shout the news, proclaim
> God's Jubilee! Jesus died to make atonement
> and set poor sinners free!'

Now when he heard that John had been arrested, he withdrew into Galilee....From that time Jesus began to preach, saying, 'Repent, for the kingdom of heaven is at hand.'

— Matthew 4:12,17 ESV

John's message was 'Repent, for the kingdom of heaven is at hand.' Herod could silence John but He couldn't silence God's messengers. Jesus took up where John left off and preached exactly the same message. 'The word of God is not bound!' (2 Tim.2:9 ESV).

I am sending you to them [the Gentiles] to open their eyes and turn them from darkness to light, and from the power of Satan to God, so that they may receive forgiveness of sins and a place among those who are sanctified by faith in me.

— Acts 26:17,18 NIV

The Gentiles were in spiritual darkness, held captive by the power of Satan. Paul's preaching would enlighten the eyes of their hearts, turning them to the light of divine truth, to be forgiven and sanctified, made pure in Christ through faith in Jesus.

Good News!

I TRY TO FIND COMMON GROUND WITH EVERYONE, DOING EVERYTHING I CAN TO SAVE SOME. I DO EVERYTHING TO SPREAD THE GOOD NEWS AND SHARE IN ITS BLESSINGS.

— 1 Corinthians 9:22,23 NLT

Paul's example is worth imitating. Without compromising the law of Christ, he made himself accessible to unbelievers, so that he could share the gospel with them. His overriding desire was to win souls for Christ, not to alienate them.

THE TESTIMONY OF JESUS IS THE SPIRIT OF PROPHECY.

— Revelation 19:10 ESV

Everything to do with Jesus Christ must be accepted by faith. The prophetic writings foretell His supernatural birth; His Deity; His atoning death and resurrection; His return to earth as King of Kings. The Word of God testifies to His Divine origin, His atoning death and resurrection, His power to forgive sins and bestow eternal life; His future glory.

GRACE

WHO IS MY MOTHER, AND WHO ARE MY BROTHERS?
POINTING TO HIS DISCIPLES, HE SAID, 'HERE ARE
MY MOTHER AND MY BROTHERS. FOR WHOEVER
DOES THE WILL OF MY FATHER IN HEAVEN IS MY
BROTHER AND SISTER AND MOTHER.'

— MATTHEW 12:48-50 NIV

What grace! This perfect One, who pleased God in everything He did, counts failing men and women like us as family, so long as we conform our lives to the will of his Father in heaven, which is revealed to us in His Word.

THE LAW WAS BROUGHT IN SO THAT THE TRESPASS MIGHT INCREASE. BUT WHERE SIN INCREASED, GRACE INCREASED ALL THE MORE.

— ROMANS 5:20 NIV

'The Law came in to make matters still worse. It substituted conscious sin for unconscious, and so heightened its guilt. But all this is more than retrieved by grace' (*Ellicott*).

NOW NO CONDEMNATION FOR THOSE WHO ARE IN CHRIST JESUS...FOR THOSE GOD FOREKNEW HE ALSO PREDESTINED TO BE CONFORMED TO THE IMAGE OF HIS SON...AND THOSE HE PREDESTINED, HE ALSO CALLED; THOSE HE CALLED, HE ALSO JUSTIFIED; THOSE HE JUSTIFIED, HE ALSO GLORIFIED.

— ROMANS 8:1,29,30 NIV

'*Who shall recall His pardon or His grace? Or who the broken chain of guilt replace?*'

Not only has God broken the chain of our guilt - by Christ's death and resurrection, He has forged for us a chain of redemption, of Sovereign Grace. All due to the One who is now exalted to the highest place in heaven!

Grace

For you know the grace of our Lord Jesus Christ, that though he was rich, yet for your sake he became poor, so that you through his poverty might become rich.

— 2 Corinthians 8:9 NIV

We measure His humility by the majesty he laid aside; we measure his poverty by the glory that was His before the world was; and we measure His grace by the way he responded to the hatred of men: *'When they hurled their insults at him, he did not retaliate; when he suffered, he made no threats.'* (1 Pet 2:23 NIV)

Greed

A FAITHFUL MAN WILL ABOUND WITH BLESSINGS, BUT WHOEVER HASTENS TO BE RICH WILL NOT GO UNPUNISHED...A STINGY MAN HASTENS AFTER WEALTH AND DOES NOT KNOW THAT POVERTY WILL COME UPON HIM...A GREEDY MAN STIRS UP STRIFE, BUT THE ONE WHO TRUSTS IN THE LORD WILL BE ENRICHED.

— PROVERBS 28:20, 22, 25 ESV

Here is a contrast of opposites. Faithfulness to God brings many blessings, not the least of which is Divine approval and spiritual wealth: but the love of money results in spiritual poverty. The Lord Jesus said *'You cannot serve God and money.'* (Matt 6:24) It's either one or the other.

Guidance

And they told David, saying, Behold, the Philistines are fighting against Keilah, and they rob the threshing-floors. Therefore David inquired of the LORD, saying, Shall I go and smite these Philistines? And the LORD said unto David, Go, and smite the Philistines, and save Keilah. And David's men said unto him, Behold, we be afraid here in Judah: how much more then if we go to Keilah against the armies of the Philistines? Then David inquired of the LORD yet again. And the LORD answered him and said, Arise, go down to Keilah; for I will deliver the Philistines into thine hand. And David and his men went to Keilah, and fought with the Philistines, and brought away their cattle, and slew therewith a great slaughter. So David saved the inhabitants of Keilah.

— 1 Samuel 23:1-5

David's example is commendable. When faced with a difficult decision, involving the lives of the others in his care, he went back to the Lord and asked 'yet again', to ensure the action he was about to take was indeed in the will of God and would be blessed of Him. From this we learn, to be doubly sure of the rightness of any significant action we may be contemplating before committing ourselves.

> *'Take time to be holy, let Him be thy Guide;*
> *And run not before Him, whatever betide.*
> *In joy or in sorrow, still follow the Lord,*
> *And, looking to Jesus, still trust in His Word.*
>
> *Take time to be holy, be calm in thy soul,*
> *Each thought and each motive beneath His*
> *control...'*

— W. D. LONGSTAFF, 1822-1894

The Holy Spirit

Not by might, nor by power, but by my Spirit, says the LORD of hosts.

— Zechariah 4:6 ESV

Zechariah saw a golden lampstand, unattended by human agency, burning brightly because of a continuous supply of oil.

The Spirit of God operates independently of human strength and is the source of unlimited divine power.

THE ADVOCATE ...WILL PROVE THE WORLD TO BE IN THE WRONG ABOUT SIN AND RIGHTEOUSNESS AND JUDGMENT...ABOUT RIGHTEOUSNESS, BECAUSE I AM GOING TO THE FATHER, WHERE YOU CAN SEE ME NO LONGER.

— JOHN 16:7-11 NIV

The Lord Jesus was the lightning rod of Truth and Love and Righteous Judgement. He thrilled, inspired and challenged those who heard Him as no other did. Now that He has returned to His Father in Heaven, The gracious Holy Spirit continues the work of Divine Grace in the hearts of men and women.

Hypocrisy

A PRIEST HAPPENED TO BE GOING DOWN THE SAME ROAD, AND WHEN HE SAW THE MAN, HE PASSED BY ON THE OTHER SIDE. SO TOO, A LEVITE.

— LUKE 10:31,32 NIV

The Priest and the Levite were 'lawkeepers', sticklers for the letter of the law. But their self-righteousness was only 'window dressing'. Their hearts were cold and hard. It was left to a despised Samaritan to show kindness and compassion to a fellow human being!

To the man who wasn't sure who his neighbour was, Jesus said: 'Go and do likewise.'

HUMILITY

THE LORD YOUR GOD IS GRACIOUS AND COMPAS-
SIONATE. HE WILL NOT TURN HIS FACE FROM YOU IF
YOU RETURN TO HIM.

— 2 CHRONICLES 30:9 NIV

God is always willing to forgive and forget.
The onus is on us, to humble ourselves, turn from our sins and return to the One who waits to bless.

> *'Who is a pardoning God like Thee?*
> *Or who has grace so rich and free?'*
>
> — (S. DAVIES)

> DOUBTLESS YOU ARE THE ONLY PEOPLE WHO MATTER, AND WISDOM WILL DIE WITH YOU!
>
> — JOB 12:2 NIV

Job's biting sarcasm highlighted the conceit of those who judged him. Solomon spoke of 'those who are pure in their own eyes' (Proverbs 30:12) The Lord called the scribes and Pharisees, 'hypocrites' (Matt 23:25). Paul wrote about some who were 'puffed up, knowing nothing.' (1 Tim 6:4). Humility is characteristic of true disciples. They are willing to listen to and learn from those who have more knowledge and experience than themselves.

> MY SACRIFICE, O GOD, IS A BROKEN SPIRIT; A BROKEN AND CONTRITE HEART YOU, GOD, WILL NOT DESPISE.
>
> — PSALM 51:17 NIV

Not one of us can boast in our own righteousness - 'see how good I am'! won't wash with God. The only sacrifice we may offer to God is that of a broken heart, of being truly sorry for our sinful nature. David's pride was broken when he realised how far away from God he had gone. When he repented of his sin, he experienced God's mercy and forgiveness, though he still faced serious consequences because of what he had done.

HUMILITY

I WILL PRAISE GOD'S NAME IN SONG AND GLORIFY HIM WITH THANKSGIVING. THIS WILL PLEASE THE LORD MORE THAN AN OX, MORE THAN A BULL WITH ITS HORNS AND HOOVES.

— PSALM 69:30,31 NIV

It's not the size of our gift that matters but the size of our appreciation of Him. God looks on the heart.

AS IF THE DEW OF HERMON WERE FALLING ON MOUNT ZION.

— PSALM 133:3 NIV

The precious oil 'ran down' on Aaron's beard and it 'came down' on his garments like the dew, which 'came down on the mountains of Zion'. The Lord Jesus came DOWN to a manger in Bethlehem; DOWN to Calvary's mountain; DOWN to the cross, to 'seek and to save' sinners like you and me, so that we could 'come unto mount Zion, and unto the city of the living God'. (Heb 12:22)

But you did not honour the God who holds in his hand your life and all your ways. ... That very night Belshazzar, king of the Babylonians, was slain.

— Daniel 5:23,3 NIV

The wisest man who ever lived wrote: 'death is the destiny of everyone; the living should take this to heart.' (Ecc. 7:2 NIV) We should live our lives in the light of eternity, knowing that we shall give account to God 'for every careless word' we speak. (Mat. 12:36 ESV)

He has shown you, O man, what is good; And what does the Lord require of you But to do justly, To love mercy, And to walk humbly with your God?

— Micah 6:8 NKJV

Our Sovereign Lord is not looking for an extravagant outward show of sacrifice or commitment. Instead, He calls for our faithful attention to the things that are central to His character: Uprightness; Kindness; Humility. *'It is the way the Master went; Should not the servant tread it still?'* (H. Bonar)

Humility

THE GREATEST AMONG YOU WILL BE YOUR SERVANT. FOR THOSE WHO EXALT THEMSELVES WILL BE HUMBLED, AND THOSE WHO HUMBLE THEMSELVES WILL BE EXALTED.

— MATTHEW 23:11,12 NIV

Unlike the scribes and Pharisees, who flaunted their position of authority, the Lord Jesus was the greatest example of the principle that those who take the lowest place in order to serve others, will be raised to a place of enduring honour and respect.

AND SHE ANSWERED AND SAID TO HIM, 'YES, LORD, YET EVEN THE LITTLE DOGS UNDER THE TABLE EAT FROM THE CHILDREN'S CRUMBS.'

— MARK 7:28 NIV

Never-mind the fact that the Jews were God's chosen people, this Gentile woman was willing to count herself of no reputation. Her answer touched the Lord's heart, for that's exactly what He Himself had done. Her humility was rewarded when He freed her daughter from Satan's power.

> For he not only accepted our appeal, but being himself very earnest he is going to you of his own accord.
>
> — 2 Corinthians 8:17 ESV

Titus was humble enough and wise enough to accept the exhortations of his brethren. Humble enough to be reasoned with and wise enough to know that he did not have a monopoly of the Spirit of God. Titus had a shepherd heart, for he earnestly sought the welfare of God's people.

> He made himself nothing by taking the very nature of a servant, being made in human likeness. And being found in appearance as a man, he humbled himself by becoming obedient to death - even death on a cross!
>
> — Philippians 2:7,8 NIV

If a monarch left the palace and came to live in a rented flat with no servants to wait on them, no chauffeur driven limousine, no cook to make their meals, we'd have a faint idea of what it meant for the King of Kings to empty himself of 'the glory that was his before the world was' and come into this world to save us.

The House of God

HE WENT FROM PLACE TO PLACE UNTIL HE CAME TO BETHEL, TO THE PLACE BETWEEN BETHEL AND AI WHERE HIS TENT HAD BEEN EARLIER AND WHERE HE HAD FIRST BUILT AN ALTAR.

— GENESIS 13:3,4 NIV

Abram returned to Bethel. He could build no altar in Egypt, for Egypt was not conducive to the worship of Jehovah. Sure, he had become wealthy in the currency of this world; but only by dwelling in the land of promise, in undivided unity with the call of God, could Abram fulfil his spiritual destiny; only there could he become 'rich in faith and inherit the kingdom' (James 2:5)

A BIBLE VERSE EACH DAY

Blessed are those who dwell in your house,
ever singing your praise! *Selah*.

— Psalm 84:4 ESV

The Psalms of the sons of Korah reflect a passionate allegiance to the House of God. Also of note is their humility: 'I would rather be a doorkeeper in the house of my God than dwell in the tents of wickedness.' (Ps 84:10) The sons of Korah knew that they were literally 'brands plucked from the burning' - they highly valued the privilege that was theirs to worship and serve in God's House - and never ever took it for granted.

The curtain of the temple was torn in two, from top to bottom.

— Matt 27:51 NIV

Israel's house was 'left unto them desolate'. The presence of God had departed. Christ's great victory on the cross meant that a new covenant temple would be built from living stones 'fitly framed together' forming a spiritual house 'for a habitation of God in the spirit'. This is what the risen Lord Jesus had in view when He said to His disciples: 'Go ye therefore, and make disciples of all the nations' (Matt 28:18,19)

Holiness

May the Lord make your love increase and overflow for each other and for everyone else... May he strengthen your hearts so that you will be blameless and holy in the presence of our God and Father when our Lord Jesus comes with all his holy ones.

— 1 Thessalonians 3:12,13 NIV

The ambition of the Christian is to be blameless and holy at the return of the Lord Jesus. May we seek His grace and power today, to cleanse us from sin and to fill our hearts to overflowing with Divine love, for the blessing of others.

INJUSTICE AND BETRAYAL

YOU...SMEAR ME WITH LIES; YOU ARE WORTHLESS PHYSICIANS, ALL OF YOU! IF ONLY YOU WOULD BE ALTOGETHER SILENT! FOR YOU, THAT WOULD BE WISDOM.

— JOB 13:4,5 NIV

Thus Job replied to the continual and unfair criticism of those who were supposed to be his 'friends'!

The story is told of a Scotsman who slipped out of a church service early. On his way down the steps of the Kirk a passing friend asked, 'Is he finished?' To which he replied 'Aye, he's finished but he'll no' stop.'

There are times when 'less is more' and 'silence is golden'!

MISERABLE COMFORTERS ARE YE ALL...MY FRIENDS SCORN ME.

— JOB 16:2,20 RV

If Job felt let down by his friends, how much more did Judas' betrayal hurt the Lord Jesus? The words of King David prefigure His experience: 'If an enemy were insulting me, I could endure it; if a foe were rising against me, I could hide. But it is you, a man like myself, my companion, my close friend with whom I once enjoyed sweet fellowship at the house of God' (Ps 55:12,13)

Integrity

They could find no corruption in him, because he was trustworthy and neither corrupt nor negligent. Finally these men said, 'We will never find any basis for charges against this man Daniel unless it has something to do with the law of his God.'

— Daniel 6:4,5 NIV

What a commendation! Could the same be said of me?

Greet Andronicus and Junia, my fellow Jews who have been in prison with me. They are outstanding among the apostles.

— Romans 16:7 NIV

'Outstanding' is not a word we use lightly. Andronicus and Junia may only be names to us, but they had such moral courage and spiritual strength, they went to prison 'for the sake of the Name'. No wonder they were held in such high esteem.

Righteous Judgement

THE GRACIOUS HAND OF OUR GOD IS ON EVERYONE WHO LOOKS TO HIM, BUT HIS GREAT ANGER IS AGAINST ALL WHO FORSAKE HIM.

— EZRA 8:22 NIV

As the father lavished love upon his 'prodigal' son (Luke 15) who returned to confess his sin, so God's heart goes out to all who return to Him - but eternal destruction awaits those who turn their backs on God's mercy. *'God cannot be mocked. A man reaps what he sows.'* (Galatians 6:7)

A BIBLE VERSE EACH DAY

It is time for you to act, Lord; your law is being broken....I consider all your precepts right.

— Psalm 119:126,128 NIV

When men abandon God's good laws and create laws which contradict God, then it is time for God to step in and judge them. In a world of increasing opposition to God's Holy word, we look for the return of the King of Kings who will restore righteous judgment and make this spiritual and moral desert 'flourish like the rose'.

∼

I will make you ... a warning and a horror, to the nations all around you, when I execute judgments on you in anger and fury, and with furious rebukes—I am the LORD; I have spoken.

— Ezekiel 5:14,15 ESV

Ezekiel was tasked with pronouncing heavy judgements on his own people. They had turned their backs on God's good laws and defiled his sanctuary; God judged them severely for their rebelliousness—and as a warning to the surrounding nations. *'God is not mocked; for whatever a man sows, that he will also reap.'* (Galatians 6:7)

∼

Righteous Judgement

> The one who sins is the one who will die. The child will not share the guilt of the parent, nor will the parent share the guilt of the child. The righteousness of the righteous will be credited to them, and the wickedness of the wicked will be charged against them.
>
> — Ezekiel 18:20 NIV

Each of us is responsible for our own actions. God will hold us accountable and will judge us according to the choices we make in life. *'God 'will repay each person according to what they have done."* (Romans 2:6)

> I also raised up prophets from among your children and Nazirites from among your youths... But you made the Nazirites drink wine and commanded the prophets not to prophesy.
>
> — Amos 2:11,12 NIV

Amos pronounced God's judgement on Israel and Judah for their extremely serious moral and spiritual violations of His laws. Not only were they doing wrong, they were deliberately cancelling the voice of God through His servants. They were sowing the wind and they would reap the whirlwind.

A BIBLE VERSE EACH DAY

When disaster comes to a city, has not the Lord caused it? Surely the Sovereign Lord does nothing without revealing his plan to his servants the prophets.

— Amos 3:6,7 NIV

In Noah's day God caused the flood. In Abraham's day He sent fire and brimstone on Sodom and Gomorrah. In Joseph's day He sent famine on the nation of Egypt. In Moses day He sent plagues. In each case, divine judgement reminded men that there is a God who holds each of us accountable for our actions.

The Lord is slow to anger but great in power; the Lord will not leave the guilty unpunished.

— Nahum 1:3 NIV

Just because divine judgement is delayed, does not mean it will never happen. In Noah's day, He waited 100 years for people to repent but finally the flood came. God earnestly desires that *'all men should be saved, and come to the knowledge of the truth'* (1 Tim. 2:4)

Righteous Judgement

> The Son of Man will send out his angels, and they will weed out of his kingdom everything that causes sin and all who do evil. They will throw them into the blazing furnace.
>
> — Matthew 13:41,42 NIV

Hell is real. The lake of fire is real. All who reject the goodness of God will experience perpetual, eternal destruction. Each person must decide for themselves whether they will go their own way or accept God's way of salvation.

> He will reply, 'Truly I tell you, whatever you did not do for one of the least of these, you did not do for me.' Then they will go away to eternal punishment, but the righteous to eternal life.
>
> — Matthew 25:45,46 NIV

At the beginning of the Lord's thousand year reign on earth, He will judge between those who have been faithful to Him and those who have turned their back on Him and His faithful ones. Each will receive the due reward of the choices they have made.

GOD RAISED HIM FROM THE DEAD ON THE THIRD DAY...HE IS THE ONE WHOM GOD APPOINTED AS JUDGE OF THE LIVING AND THE DEAD...EVERYONE WHO BELIEVES IN HIM RECEIVES FORGIVENESS OF SINS THROUGH HIS NAME.

— ACTS 10:40-43 NIV

Every one of us will stand before Jesus Christ. He will assess our lives in the light of our attitude towards Him. Those who trust Him as Saviour will be forgiven. Those who trust in their own righteousness will be condemned.

I WATCHED AS THE LAMB OPENED THE FIRST OF THE SEVEN SEALS.

— REVELATION 6:1 NIV

Revelation chapter 6 tells us what will happen when six of the seven seals are opened. We are given a preview of the events that will take place when divine judgements fall on a rebellious world. How solemn, that it is the newly slain Lamb who begins this programme of God's final dealings with those who hate Him.

Righteous Judgement

My conscience is clear, but that does not make me innocent. It is the Lord who judges me. Therefore judge nothing before the appointed time; wait until the Lord comes. He will bring to light what is hidden in darkness and will expose the motives of the heart. At that time each will receive their praise from God.

— 1 Corinthians 4:4,5 NIV

The Lord looks on the heart. He sees past the smokescreens of hypocrisy and self-justification that we put up to convince ourselves we are right. One day He will expose our innermost secrets, and judge accordingly.

JUSTICE

> THEY MADE THEIR HEARTS DIAMOND-HARD LEST THEY SHOULD HEAR THE LAW AND THE WORDS THAT THE LORD OF HOSTS HAD SENT ... 'AS I CALLED, AND THEY WOULD NOT HEAR, SO THEY CALLED, AND I WOULD NOT HEAR,' SAYS THE LORD OF HOSTS.
>
> — ZECHARIAH 7:12,13 ESV

Israel's refusal to listen made God so angry, He uprooted them for seventy years. If we refuse to listen to God when He calls, He will refuse to listen when we need Him. Those who think they can turn on God's compassion like a tap, soon find He is not a soft touch.

Justification

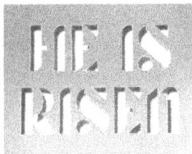

> But whoever does what is true comes to the light, so that it may be clearly seen that his works have been carried out in God.
>
> — John 3:21 ESV

The only 'works' that can be 'carried out in God' are works of faith. Works of proud independence cannot be owned by God; the only works which God can accept from guilt-ridden sinners, are those that demonstrate complete reliance on His power to redeem us, on His provision for our spiritual birth, namely, faith in the Saviour who came from heaven to die on the cross, to take away our guilt.

> THAT HE MIGHT BE JUST AND THE JUSTIFIER OF THE ONE WHO HAS FAITH IN JESUS.
>
> — ROMANS 3:26 ESV

By faith we understand the marvellous logic of Divine Grace.

But it is much harder to comprehend the enormous personal cost of our redemption:

'why have you forsaken me?' (Matt 27:46) What desperate words are these, coming from the lips of Deity! Perhaps we can begin to understand what it cost Him to redeem our lost souls and restore communion between God and man.

He restored that communion at the expense of His own.

∽

> HE WAS FULLY CONVINCED THAT GOD IS ABLE TO DO WHATEVER HE PROMISES. AND BECAUSE OF ABRAHAM'S FAITH, GOD COUNTED HIM AS RIGHTEOUS.
>
> — ROMANS 4:21,22 NLT

God keeps His promises. If He says something, He means it. In Christ, God has promised to save all who trust Him, from eternal destruction. Believing this glorifies God and vindicates His integrity. He will NEVER let you down.

∽

Justification

> He was delivered over to death for our sins and was raised to life for our justification.
>
> — Romans 4:25 NIV)

The resurrection of Christ involves the justification of those who have put their faith in Him. 'Justification' is a legal word. It means acquittal. The character of the person who was in the dock is legally vindicated and they are counted innocent. This is what the resurrection of Christ has done for the believer.

> I do not set aside the grace of God, for if righteousness could be gained through the law, Christ died for nothing!
>
> — Galatians 2:21 NIV

If 'being good' and 'doing good' cancelled out the times when we aren't quite as good as we'd like, then we would have something to boast about. Unfortunately, God cannot ignore the rottenness at the core of human nature. That's why Jesus had to die. He bore our sins, so that when by faith we rest on His finished work of redemption, God imputes the perfect righteousness of Christ to us.

THE COMING KING

HE TO WHOM IT BELONGS SHALL COME AND THE
OBEDIENCE OF THE NATIONS SHALL BE HIS.

— GENESIS 49:10 NIV

'*The crown will not be restored until he to whom it rightfully belongs shall come; to him I will give it.*' (Ezekiel 21:27 NIV)

'*you, Bethlehem Ephrathah ... out of you will come for me one who will be ruler over Israel, whose origins are from of old ...*' (Micah 5:2 NIV)

The king is coming. The nations of this world will never be right until they bow to the authority of the king they nailed to the cross.

A BIBLE VERSE EACH DAY

In his days shall the righteous flourish, And abundance of peace, till the moon be no more. He shall have dominion also from sea to sea, And from the River unto the ends of the earth.

— Psalm 72:7-8 RV

Yes, the day is coming when the oppressive policies of those who have no love of God's truth will be reversed and those who love righteousness will be exalted above those whose moral compass is broken. The result will be 'Peace on earth'.

> *'Jesus shall reign where'er the sun*
> *Does its successive journeys run,*
> *His kingdom stretch from shore to shore,*
> *Till moons shall wax and wane no more.'*

— Isaac Watts, 1674-1748

The Coming King

The Lord reigns, he is robed in majesty; the Lord is robed in majesty and armed with strength.

— Psalm 93:1 NIV

As the Lord Jesus Christ stood before Pontius Pilate, crowned with thorns and dressed in a scarlet robe, the Roman governor became acutely aware of His intrinsic OMNIPOTENCE and was even more afraid. The honour, the dignity, the unmistakable majesty of the King of Kings could not be hidden.

Kings will shut their mouths because of him. For what they were not told, they will see, and what they have not heard, they will understand.

— Isaiah 52:15 NIV

The one who 'was so disfigured beyond any human being' (v14) will return to reign as King of Kings and Lord of Lords. The grandiose ambitions of this world's rulers will be brought to nothing. They will be rendered speechless when the Saviour they rejected takes the sceptre of power from their hands.

BEHOLD, THE MAN WHOSE NAME IS THE BRANCH!
... HE SHALL BUILD THE TEMPLE OF THE LORD ... HE
SHALL BEAR THE GLORY, AND SHALL SIT AND RULE
ON HIS THRONE; SO HE SHALL BE A PRIEST ON HIS
THRONE.

— ZECHARIAH 6:12,13 NKJV

The man whose name is the BRANCH is 'the root and the offspring of David' (Rev. 22:16; cf Is. 11:1). The Lord Jesus will make the temple at Jerusalem the centre of the worship of God; He will rule this world as King and Priest and the result will be universal peace and harmony.

BEHOLD, YOUR KING IS COMING TO YOU; HE IS JUST
AND HAVING SALVATION, LOWLY AND RIDING ON A
DONKEY, A COLT, THE FOAL OF A DONKEY ... HE
SHALL SPEAK PEACE TO THE NATIONS.

— ZECHARIAH 9:9,10 NKJV

The first part of this prophecy was fulfilled when the Lord Jesus rode on a donkey from the Mount of Olives into Jerusalem, to be crucified. The second part will be fulfilled when He returns to the Mount of Olives on a white horse to establish His worldwide kingdom of peace for 1000 years.

The Coming King

> Then shall the LORD go forth, and fight against those nations, as when he fought in the day of battle. And his feet shall stand in that day upon the mount of Olives.
>
> — Zechariah 14:3,4 RV

Revelation 19 details this dramatic event. The heavens open and the majestic person whose name is the Word of God and KING OF KINGS AND LORD OF LORDS, descends to earth, followed by the armies of heaven. With a word He destroys the beast and the world's armies.

> Then will appear the sign of the Son of Man in heaven. And then all the peoples of the earth will mourn when they see the Son of Man coming on the clouds of heaven, with power and great glory.
>
> — Mathew 24:30 NIV

When? At the end of the antichrist's reign of terror, the Lord Jesus will be revealed as King of Kings and Lord of Lords, followed by the armies of heaven. He will throw the beast and the false prophet alive into the lake of fire, and kill the armies of the world with his voice. (Rev. 19)

THE ANGEL SAID TO THEM, 'DO NOT BE AFRAID. I BRING YOU GOOD NEWS THAT WILL CAUSE GREAT JOY FOR ALL THE PEOPLE. TODAY IN THE TOWN OF DAVID A SAVIOUR HAS BEEN BORN TO YOU; HE IS THE MESSIAH, THE LORD.

— LUKE 2:10,11 NIV

As we celebrate the first coming of the Son of God to earth, it is great to look forward to the day when He will come again - not as a helpless baby, not to go to the cross - but *'with power and great glory'* (Matthew 24:30) to reign as *'King of Kings and Lord of Lords.'* (Revelation 19:16)

SUDDENLY TWO MEN DRESSED IN WHITE STOOD BESIDE THEM. 'MEN OF GALILEE,' THEY SAID, 'WHY DO YOU STAND HERE LOOKING INTO THE SKY? THIS SAME JESUS, WHO HAS BEEN TAKEN FROM YOU INTO HEAVEN, WILL COME BACK IN THE SAME WAY YOU HAVE SEEN HIM GO INTO HEAVEN.

— ACTS 1:10,11 NIV

He's coming back! First of all, to the air (1 Thess 4) to call his saved ones home to heaven, then as King of Kings to the Mount of Olives (Zech 14:4) to judge the world in righteousness and usher in a thousand years of peace. Are you looking forward to the second advent of the 'Prince of Peace?'

The Coming King

HE SHALL RULE THEM WITH A ROD OF IRON.

— REVELATION 19:15 RV

When the King of Kings returns to earth, He will find a world full of people who have so many ideas contrary to God's thinking that they will not naturally bow to His will. They will be forced to accept HIS way of doing things until the benefits of His munificent rule become apparent:

> *People and realms of every tongue*
> *dwell on his love with sweetest song,*
> *and infant voices shall proclaim*
> *their early blessings on his name.*
>
> — ISAAC WATTS, 1674-1748

> *So be it, Lord! Thy throne shall never,*
> *Like earth's proud empires, pass away;*
> *Thy kingdom stands and grows forever*
> *Till all Thy creatures own Thy sway.*
>
> — JOHN ELLERTON, 1826-1893

KINDNESS AND GENEROSITY

AND GOD GAVE SOLOMON ...LARGENESS OF HEART.

— 1 KINGS 4:29 R.V.

Solomon had a generous heart. During his reign he freely shared his wisdom and understanding to the benefit of Israel and the surrounding nations. However, the Lord Jesus displayed largeness of heart beyond anything Solomon ever could, because He wasn't shackled by a flawed human nature. He was God incarnate. Everything He did was motivated by Divine love. His largeness of heart has benefitted us for all eternity.

A BIBLE VERSE EACH DAY

>SHE OPENS HER MOUTH WITH WISDOM, AND THE TEACHING OF KINDNESS IS ON HER TONGUE.
>
>— PROVERBS 31:26 ESV

The word 'kindness' in this verse is the Hebrew word *'checed'*. It is often translated as lovingkindness or mercy when describing God's dealings with His people. Dr Strong suggests it can also imply our piety or goodness towards God. The apostle James, writing to born again believers, expands these thoughts further: 'the wisdom that comes from heaven is first of all pure; then peace-loving, considerate, submissive, full of mercy and good fruit, impartial and sincere.' James 3:17)

∾

>DO TO OTHERS WHAT YOU WOULD HAVE THEM DO TO YOU, FOR THIS SUMS UP THE LAW AND THE PROPHETS.
>
>— MATTHEW 7:12 NIV

How would I like others to treat me? With courtesy and respect, with kindness and compassion, by being a good neighbour, willing to help but not obstructive or a nuisance or difficult. *'Go and do thou likewise.'*

∾

KINDNESS AND GENEROSITY

> NOW JESUS LOVED MARTHA AND HER SISTER AND LAZARUS.
>
> — JOHN 11:5 NIV

The Lord's friendship with this family began when 'Martha received him into her house.' (Luke 10:38) It was Martha who first recognised His worth. Together with her brother and sister they opened their hearts and their house to him. He was always welcome in Bethany! How much their kindness and hospitality meant to Him who was 'despised and rejected of men...'

Kingdom, Christ's Millennial Kingdom

You will go out in joy and be led forth in peace; the mountains and hills will burst into song before you, and all the trees of the field will clap their hands. Instead of the thornbush will grow the juniper, and instead of briers the myrtle will grow. This will be for the Lord's renown, for an everlasting sign, that will endure forever.

— Isaiah 55:12,13 NIV

A glorious time of joy, peace and abundant life lies ahead for this world. The effects of sin will be suppressed, God's ancient people Israel will flourish and every nation will enjoy the lasting benefits of Messiah's reign.

> They will rebuild the ancient ruins and restore the places long devastated; they will renew the ruined cities that have been devastated for generations.
>
> — Isaiah 61:4 NIV

What has been lost for generations will be rebuilt. Not simply bricks and mortar but also, the moral and spiritual character of God's holy nation. Israel will acknowledge Christ as King of Kings and Lord of Lords. The best is yet to be!

> The wolf and the lamb will feed together, and the lion will eat straw like the ox, and dust will be the serpent's food. They will neither harm nor destroy on all my holy mountain, says the Lord.
>
> — Isaiah 65:25 NIV

We can hardly imagine a world where wild animals will be so tame that parents allow their children to play with them. A world where fear of injury is removed and the potential of every living thing can flourish. God will see to it that His original vision for this world becomes reality.

> 'The days are coming,' declares the Lord, 'when ... I will bring my people Israel back from exile. 'They will rebuild the ruined cities and live in them. They will plant vineyards and drink their wine; they will make gardens and eat their fruit. I will plant Israel in their own land, never again to be uprooted from the land I have given them,' says the Lord your God.
>
> — Amos 9:13-15 NIV

In the millennial reign of Christ, instead of suffering 'hell on earth', the redeemed of Israel will enjoy one thousand years of heaven on earth.

> They will beat their swords into plowshares and their spears into pruning hooks. Nation will not take up sword against nation, nor will they train for war anymore.
>
> — Micah 4:3 NIV

Jesus, the Son of God, will reign over this world for a thousand years, as King of Kings and Lord of Lords. His reign will be characterised by such peace and prosperity that there will be no more wars, no more need for armies of soldiers, no more wanton destruction and killing. The manufacture of agricultural tools will replace the weapons of war. How wonderful time will that be!

> Everyone will sit under their own vine and under their own fig tree, and no one will make them afraid, for the Lord Almighty has spoken.
>
> — Micah 4:4 NIV

Micah's prophetic vision describes normal life during the soon coming millennial reign of Christ on this earth. It's a picture of universal contentment and security; a world where no-one need lock their doors at night. Come quickly Lord Jesus!

> For the earth will be filled with the knowledge of the glory of the Lord as the waters cover the sea.
>
> — Habakkuk 2:14 NIV

God gave Habakkuk a vision of a glorious time ahead, when the whole world will be blessed by the exaltation of the man of Calvary to global power and authority. Then, God's creation will finally reach its spiritual, physical and economic potential. *Lord Jesus, please come soon!*

Laziness

A LITTLE EXTRA SLEEP, A LITTLE MORE SLUMBER, A LITTLE FOLDING OF THE HANDS TO REST— THEN POVERTY WILL POUNCE ON YOU LIKE A BANDIT; SCARCITY WILL ATTACK YOU LIKE AN ARMED ROBBER.

— Proverbs 24:33,34 NLT

This is about the habits we form. If we get lazy and start to give in to the temptation to avoid work and take it easy, the danger is it will become a mindset, a habitual shirking of responsibility. The result of this is poverty - poverty which robs us not only of enough money to make ends meet but a poverty of mind and spirit.

MY PEOPLE ARE DESTROYED FROM LACK OF KNOWLEDGE. 'BECAUSE YOU HAVE REJECTED KNOWLEDGE, I ALSO REJECT YOU.'

— HOSEA 4:6 NIV

Ignorance can be remedied. Wilful ignorance is far more serious. Disciples of Christ ought to have an appetite for 'the whole counsel of God' (Acts 20:27), not just the bits that immediately appeal.

The Light of Life

God has delivered me from going down to the pit, and I shall live to enjoy the light of life.

— Job 33:28 NIV

It is God who in mercy, rescues people from the consequences of their sin: the awful darkness of a lost eternity in the Lake of Fire. He sent His beloved Son to die so that we could enjoy the light of eternal life. Jesus said: *'Whoever follows me will never walk in darkness, but will have the light of life'* (John 8:12 NIV).

> I AM THE LIGHT OF THE WORLD. WHOEVER FOLLOWS ME WILL NEVER WALK IN DARKNESS, BUT WILL HAVE THE LIGHT OF LIFE.
>
> — JOHN 8:12 NIV

Perhaps in the ceaseless ages of eternity, as we learn the stories of our co-redeemed, we will begin to get some understanding of what it cost the Lord Jesus Christ to rescue us from moral and spiritual darkness and call us into *'his marvellous light.'* (1 Pet 2:9).

LIVING WATER

NO ONE CAN ENTER THE KINGDOM OF GOD UNLESS
THEY ARE BORN OF WATER AND THE SPIRIT.

— JOHN 3:5 NIV

The Lord Jesus spoke to Nicodemus about the water of the Word of God. This is the same water He spoke about with the woman at Sychars well - living water, *'springing up unto eternal life'* -*'For you have been born again...through the living and enduring word of God'* (1 Pet 1:23 NIV).

A BIBLE VERSE EACH DAY

Jesus said to the servants, 'Fill the jars with water' ... the master of the banquet ... called the bridegroom aside and said, 'You have saved the best till now.'

— John 2:6-10 NIV

CANA

They were feasting with their comrades,
Tasting pleasures, one by one,
But they knew not One among them,
Was their Saviour, God's own Son.
And, like all of earth that charms us,
As the rose by garden wall,
When the flower is full and fragrant,
Soon the petals shrink and fall.
'So, like all of earthly pleasure,
Soon their vessels empty stand,
But there's One alone can help them,
If they will do His command.
See them bring their vessels to Him,
Fill with water clear and fine,
Look to Christ now, in amazement,
Lo! The water turns to wine!
Oh, how joyful now they taste it,
'Tis the best they ever had,
Sweeter far than any other,
Now they're satisfied and glad.'

— Ellen Jean Bairnson, of Brakes, Dunrossness, Shetland. (1903-1975

Living Water

Whoever drinks of this water will thirst again, but whoever drinks of the water that I shall give him will never thirst. But the water that I shall give him will become in him a fountain of water springing up into everlasting life.

— John 4:13,14 NKJV

The woman had been drinking from a well that could never satisfy. Five husbands and counting. But then she met the Messiah! He spoke to her of true worship and communion with God, of a spiritual life emanating from the everlasting wellspring of divine love.

DIVINE LOVE

BUT TO YOU WHO ARE LISTENING I SAY: LOVE YOUR ENEMIES, DO GOOD TO THOSE WHO HATE YOU, BLESS THOSE WHO CURSE YOU, PRAY FOR THOSE WHO MISTREAT YOU...DO TO OTHERS AS YOU WOULD HAVE THEM DO TO YOU.

— LUKE 6:27-31 NIV

Jesus instructed His followers to respond to provocation by doing the exact opposite of their natural instincts. Loving those who hate us, being kind to those who've been unkind to us, doesn't come naturally. It's easy to be nice to those who like us. We need divine power to show the same consideration to our enemies.

A BIBLE VERSE EACH DAY

I LAY DOWN MY LIFE—ONLY TO TAKE IT UP AGAIN. NO ONE TAKES IT FROM ME, BUT I LAY IT DOWN OF MY OWN ACCORD.

— JOHN 10:17,18 NIV

Jesus voluntarily laid down His life. It was not the nails that bound Him to the cross, neither was it the machinations of Israel's corrupt and godless leaders or the might of Roman power that forced Him to die: IT WAS HIS LOVE FOR US that brought Him all the way from heaven's throne to intentionally give His life, 'the righteous for the unrighteous, that he might bring us to God' (1 Pet 3:18 ESV)

GREATER LOVE HATH NO MAN THAN THIS THAT A MAN LAY DOWN HIS LIFE FOR HIS FRIENDS.

— JOHN 15:13 RV

Natural love usually stops short at dying for our friends. At a stretch some would even give their life for a good person. But the love of God goes far beyond our meagre affections: 'God shows his love for us in that while we were still sinners, Christ died for us....' (Rom 5:8 ESV)

Divine Love

Love...is not easily angered, it keeps no record of wrongs.

— 1 Corinthians 13:4,5 NIV

They stripped him and put a scarlet robe on him, and then twisted together a crown of thorns and set it on his head...'Hail, king of the Jews!' they said. They spit on him, and took the staff and struck him on the head again and again *(Matthew 27:28-30)*.

Jesus said, 'Father, forgive them, for they do not know what they are doing' (Luke 23:34).

~

Now may the Lord direct your hearts into the love of God and into the patience of Christ.

— 2 Thessalonians 3:5 NKJV

Christian love, whether exercised toward the brethren, or toward men generally, is not an impulse from the feelings, it does not always run with the natural inclinations, nor does it spend itself only upon those for whom some affinity is discovered...love seeks opportunity to do good to all men.

(*Vine's Expository Dictionary of NT Words*)

~

SACRIFICIAL LOVE

> YOUR SERVANT GUARANTEED THE BOY'S SAFETY TO MY FATHER...NOW THEN, PLEASE LET YOUR SERVANT REMAIN HERE AS MY LORD'S SLAVE IN PLACE OF THE BOY, AND LET THE BOY RETURN WITH HIS BROTHERS.
>
> — GENESIS 44:32,33 NIV

Judah loved Jacob and Benjamin so much that he was willing to forfeit his freedom so that they could be reunited. His sacrificial love broke down the barrier of Joseph's stern justice and opened the floodgates of mercy toward his guilty brothers. Here is a lovely picture of Christ's sacrificial love and Divine mercy toward us.

BUT RUTH REPLIED, 'DON'T URGE ME TO LEAVE YOU OR TO TURN BACK FROM YOU. WHERE YOU GO I WILL GO, AND WHERE YOU STAY I WILL STAY. YOUR PEOPLE WILL BE MY PEOPLE AND YOUR GOD MY GOD. WHERE YOU DIE I WILL DIE, AND THERE I WILL BE BURIED. MAY THE LORD DEAL WITH ME, BE IT EVER SO SEVERELY, IF EVEN DEATH SEPARATES YOU AND ME.'

— (RUTH 1:16,17 NIV

W as there ever a more beautiful statement of loyalty and love made or recorded anywhere? It came from Ruth's heart and shows how much being numbered with the people of Naomi's God meant to her.

HE OFFERED HER SOME ROASTED GRAIN. SHE ATE ALL SHE WANTED AND HAD SOME LEFT OVER.

— RUTH 2:14 NIV

B oaz had a soft spot for Ruth – he told the young men to let her glean among the sheaves and to pull out 'handfuls on purpose' for her to glean. He took a personal interest in her welfare. The Lord Jesus Christ had such a personal interest in our eternal welfare that He endured the cross, made atonement for our sins and rose again for our justification.

Sacrificial Love

He sends out his word, and melts them; he makes his wind blow and the waters flow.

— Psalm 147:18 ESV

This is true in the spiritual as well as the physical realm. The Lord Jesus said to Nicodemus: *'The wind blows wherever it pleases... So it is with everyone born of the Spirit.'* (John 3:8)

Hatred stirs up conflict, but love covers over all wrongs.

— Proverbs 10:12 NIV

Hatred is divisive. It causes alienation, isolation and polarisation instead of promoting unity, kindness and fellowship. Disciples of Christ strive to 'be at peace with all men', to love their neighbour and maintain good relationships so that they may win them for Christ.

A BIBLE VERSE EACH DAY

Morning by morning he awakens; he awakens my ear to hear as those who are taught.

— Isaiah 50:4 ESV

He taught huge crowds, He thrilled their hearts with wonderful words of life, with the good news of God's purposes of grace to all mankind; He awoke one morning to the knowledge that He would be arrested, falsely accused flogged, mocked, treated like a fool and then crucified. He knew He would be forsaken by God because of our sins, yet He went through with it. Such love 'demands our heart, our life, our all'.

Serve one another humbly in love. For the entire law is fulfilled in keeping this one command: 'Love your neighbour as yourself.'

— Galatians 5:13,14 NIV

The Lord Jesus told His disciples that their love for each other was the unique feature, that, in the eyes of the world, would mark them out as His followers. A love that rises above the petty jealousies and self-interest which dogs the footsteps of all whose hearts are not transformed by Christ's *agape* love.

Sacrificial Love

'Honour your father and mother'—which is the first commandment with a promise— 'so that it may go well with you and that you may enjoy long life on the earth.'

— Ephesians 6:2,3 NIV

While a healthy diet and regular exercise are important for our wellbeing, we also need to remember that long life also depends on the respect and consideration we give to our parents. Jesus set us the perfect example by honouring both His Heavenly Father and his earthly parents.

LOVE OF THE WORLD

WHOEVER LOVES HIS LIFE LOSES IT, AND WHOEVER HATES HIS LIFE IN THIS WORLD WILL KEEP IT FOR ETERNAL LIFE.

— JOHN 12:25 ESV

Judas loved his life & lost it - he loved money more than the Saviour who came to die for him. The rich young man in Matthew 19 was upright and very religious but went away sorrowful because he loved things more than he loved God. His life was lost because he turned away from the Son of God, the only person who can make us spiritually alive and give purpose and meaning to life.

Loyalty

Thus the children of Israel were subdued at that time; and the children of Judah prevailed, because they relied on the Lord God of their fathers.

— 2 Chronicles 13:18 NKJV

Led by Abijah, the children of Judah defeated the northern tribes under Jeroboam. They overcame them because they remained faithful to the worship of God in the sanctuary at Jerusalem and did not forsake God for the worship of false gods, as Israel had done. Because they remained true to the LORD, He gave the victory to them.

A BIBLE VERSE EACH DAY

Let us also go, that we may die with him.

— John 11:16 NIV

Thomas 'put all his eggs in Jesus basket'! In effect he said the same as Ittai: 'As the LORD lives, and as my lord the king lives, wherever my lord the king shall be, whether for death or for life, there also will your servant be." (2 Sam 15:21 ESV) In the day of His rejection, the Lord surely values our loyalty at least as much as the loyalty of these two men was precious to their Lord and King.

Mercy

Abigail...fell at his feet and said: '...When the Lord has fulfilled for my lord every good thing he promised...my lord will not have on his conscience the staggering burden ... of having avenged himself'... David said to Abigail, 'Praise be to the Lord, the God of Israel, who has sent you today to meet me.'

— (1 Samuel 25:23-32 NIV

Five times over, Abigail mentions 'the LORD' - she reminded David that the LORD was on his side and would keep His promises. Abigail appealed to David's reverence for the LORD and His law. How grateful David was for her timely intervention!

MUSIC: OF HEAVEN AND OF MEN

AND I SAW SOMETHING LIKE A SEA OF GLASS MINGLED WITH FIRE, AND THOSE WHO HAVE THE VICTORY OVER THE BEAST, OVER HIS IMAGE AND OVER HIS MARK AND OVER THE NUMBER OF HIS NAME...HAVING HARPS OF GOD. THEY SING THE SONG OF MOSES, THE SERVANT OF GOD, AND THE SONG OF THE LAMB.

— REVELATION 15:2,3 NKJV

These harps are not man-made. They are of Divine origin and design. What sublime music they will produce! How perfectly their melody will complement the paean of praise that arises from the hearts of that victorious multitude, who overcome such fearful odds 'by the blood of the Lamb'.

A BIBLE VERSE EACH DAY

THE ANGEL SHOWED ME THE RIVER OF THE WATER OF LIFE, AS CLEAR AS CRYSTAL, FLOWING FROM THE THRONE OF GOD AND OF THE LAMB.

— REVELATION 22:1 NIV

When Johnny Cash was 12, his older brother Jack had a dreadful accident in a sawmill. The family gathered round his hospital bed. He suddenly became lucid and said: 'I'm glad you're all here.' He closed his eyes: 'It's a beautiful river. It's going two ways; no I'm not going that way; yes, that's the way I'm going. Aww Momma, can't you see it?' His mother said 'No'. 'Well can you hear the angels?' 'No son, I can't.' 'I wish you could, they're so beautiful...It's so wonderful and what a beautiful place that I'm going.' Those were his last words.

OBEDIENCE

I will be with you.

— Genesis 31:3 NIV

If God says 'I will be with you', that's all we need to know! If we have His presence, we can go on with a good conscience, knowing that He will guide and bring us through. But, we can only expect God's presence and protection when we align ourselves with His will:

'them that honour me I will honour, and they that despise me shall be lightly esteemed.' (1 Sam 2:30)

A MAN OF BETHLEHEM IN JUDAH WENT TO SOJOURN IN THE COUNTRY OF MOAB, HE AND HIS WIFE AND HIS TWO SONS.

— RUTH 1:1 ESV

Testing times reveal true character. Contrast Elimelech and Naomi's response with that of Boaz. The famine only strengthened Boaz's resolve to continue steadfastly in the place God had given him. Naomi and Elimilech thought there was no future in Israel. They thought they could 'sojourn' and return when things improved. Bethlehem to Moab may have been easy going - but it was downhill all the way!

LEAVE HERE, TURN EASTWARD AND HIDE.

— 1 KINGS 17:3 NIV

Elijah might have said 'Hide myself? I've just arrived! Surely I should stay and see this through?' But Elijah knew his God well enough not to question Him; if God said 'go and speak', he did so; if God said hide, Elijah hid, because he had learned the importance of unquestioning obedience to the word of God.

'Trust and Obey, for there's no other way, to be happy in Jesus but to trust and obey.'

Obedience

THREE TIMES A DAY HE GOT DOWN ON HIS KNEES AND PRAYED, GIVING THANKS TO HIS GOD, JUST AS HE HAD DONE BEFORE.

— Daniel 6:19 NIV)

Even though an official decree prohibited Daniel from praying to God, he continued giving thanks to God 'just as he had done before.' When forced to make such a choice, 'we must obey God rather than men.' (Acts 5:29 ESV)

PERMIT IT TO BE SO NOW, FOR THUS IT IS FITTING FOR US TO FULFIL ALL RIGHTEOUSNESS.

— (Mattew 3:15 NKJV

Jesus submitted himself to the symbol of death and resurrection. As he came up out of the Jordan, the Spirit of God descended as a dove and rested on Him. The voice of God thundered out: 'This is My beloved Son, in whom I am well pleased.' Father, Son and Holy Spirit, united in their commitment to the divine plan for our redemption.

> MOVED WITH PITY, HE ... TOUCHED HIM AND SAID TO HIM, 'I WILL; BE CLEAN.' AND IMMEDIATELY THE LEPROSY LEFT HIM, AND HE WAS MADE CLEAN. AND JESUS STERNLY CHARGED HIM ... 'SEE THAT YOU SAY NOTHING TO ANYONE, BUT GO, SHOW YOURSELF TO THE PRIEST AND OFFER FOR YOUR CLEANSING WHAT MOSES COMMANDED, FOR A PROOF TO THEM.' BUT HE WENT OUT AND BEGAN TO TALK FREELY ABOUT IT, AND TO SPREAD THE NEWS, SO THAT JESUS COULD NO LONGER OPENLY ENTER A TOWN
>
> — MARK 1:41-45 ESV

The man ignored Jesus' instruction. His well-meaning but misguided enthusiasm made it harder for the Lord to do His work. He also missed the opportunity to provide the religious establishment with incontrovertible evidence that the Lord Jesus was doing the work of God. The words of Samuel come to mind: 'Behold, to obey is better than sacrifice, and to listen than the fat of rams.' (1 Sam. 15:22 ESV)

Obedience

> Even Gentiles, who do not have God's written law, show that they know his law when they instinctively obey it, even without having heard it.
>
> — Romans 2:14 NLT

The older versions say the Gentiles were 'a law unto themselves'. Paul reminds us that apart from external laws, God has given each of us a conscience which regulates our behaviour. God will judge each of us according to how we respond to the light He has given us.

> And we know that to them that love God all things work together for good, *even* to them that are called according to *His* purpose.
>
> — Romans 8:28 RV

There are two qualifiers in this verse: loving God and being called according to His purpose. We cannot expect all things to work together for good unless our affections are toward Him and unless we are willing to answer His call to worship in accordance with His Word.

> SON THOUGH HE WAS, HE LEARNED OBEDIENCE FROM WHAT HE SUFFERED.
>
> — HEBREWS 5:8 NIV

The Lord Jesus never had to learn how to become obedient, because there was no sin in him: His 'meat and drink' was 'to do the will of him that sent him'. But by bitter, first hand experience, He learned what obeying his Father's will meant in a world that hated Him; He learned the personal cost of obedience.

Patience

God told Pharaoh, 'I have appointed you for the very purpose of displaying my power in you and to spread my fame throughout the earth.'...even though God has the right to show his anger and his power, he is very patient with those on whom his anger falls.

— Romans 9:17,22 NLT

God wants us to acknowledge Him as our Creator. We exist because of Him. By bowing to His authority we place ourselves under His protection. If we go our own way, we place ourselves outside His mercy. God is *'slow to anger'* (Ex. 34:6) but must judge us according to the choices we make.

Peace

Who has gathered the wind in his fists? Who has wrapped up the waters in a garment? ... What is his name, and what is his son's name? Surely you know!

— Proverbs 30:4 ESV

It was the Son of God, who said to the storm 'Peace, be still'. He also endured the storm of God's wrath against our sin and 'made peace through the blood of his cross.' (Col 1:20)

In our storm tossed world we hear Him say: *'Peace I leave with you; my peace I give to you. Not as the world gives do I give to you. Let not your hearts be troubled, neither let them be afraid.'* (John 14:27)

JESUS SAID TO THE WOMAN, 'YOUR FAITH HAS SAVED YOU; GO IN PEACE.'

— LUKE 7:50 NIV

In the original Greek, the exact meaning of the phrase 'go in peace' is 'go into peace'. In Luke 7, a woman who life was a chaotic mess, falls at Jesus feet and surrenders her broken life to Him. He says 'Your sins are forgiven', and in that moment, she passes from death into life, from chaos into peace.

DO NOT BE ANXIOUS ABOUT ANYTHING, BUT IN EVERYTHING BY PRAYER AND SUPPLICATION WITH THANKSGIVING LET YOUR REQUESTS BE MADE KNOWN TO GOD. AND THE PEACE OF GOD, WHICH SURPASSES ALL UNDERSTANDING, WILL GUARD YOUR HEARTS AND YOUR MINDS IN CHRIST JESUS.

— EPHESIANS 4:6,7 ESV

Only through earnest prayer—with thanksgiving—will we be liberated from anxiety and worry. Only then will 'the peace of God' protect our hearts and minds 'in Christ Jesus'. It defies human logic but is a sublime reality for those who do it.

Prayer

SPREAD THE CORNER OF YOUR GARMENT OVER ME, SINCE YOU ARE A GUARDIAN-REDEEMER OF OUR FAMILY.

— RUTH 3:9 NIV

The Hebrew word for 'wing' ('skirt' in some versions) is here translated as 'the corner of the garment'.

When Jesus longed to gather Israel, 'as a hen gathers her brood 'under her wings' (Mat. 23:37), they rejected Him. He came into this world and died to be our guardian-redeemer. Have you ever fallen at His feet, as Ruth did at Boaz's feet, and said: *Jesus my redeemer; please spread your protective wings over me?*'

> THEY WERE HELPED IN FIGHTING THEM...BECAUSE THEY CRIED OUT TO HIM DURING THE BATTLE. HE ANSWERED THEIR PRAYERS, BECAUSE THEY TRUSTED IN HIM.
>
> — (1 CHRONICLES 5:20 NIV

In the battles of life, it is good to know we have a God who hears and answers the prayers of those who 'believe that he exists and that he rewards those who earnestly seek him.' (Heb 11:6 NIV)

~

> RISE UP; THIS MATTER IS IN YOUR HANDS. WE WILL SUPPORT YOU, SO TAKE COURAGE AND DO IT.
>
> — EZRA 10:4 NIV

In answer to Ezra's prayer, the Spirit of God moved the leaders of the people to pledge their support to Ezra in this moment of crisis. God stepped in and solved what appeared to be an insurmountable problem.

> *'Prayer...moves the hand that moves the world,*
> *To bring salvation down.'*
>
> — J. A. WALLACE

Prayer

> Since the first day that you set your mind to gain understanding and to humble yourself before your God, your words were heard.
>
> — Daniel 10:12 NIV

Prayer is never a waste of time. When we humbly seek to know and understand the will of God, He will hear us and reveal His will to us: *'If you hold to my teaching, you are really my disciples. Then you will know the truth, and the truth will set you free.'* (John 8:31,32)

> 'Simon,' he said to Peter, 'are you asleep? Couldn't you keep watch for one hour? Watch and pray so that you will not fall into temptation. The spirit is willing, but the flesh is weak.'
>
> — Mark 14:37,38 NIV

This rebuke is particularly significant in the light of Peter's actions later that night, when he denied his Lord three times. If he had followed his Master's example and prayed instead of sleeping, he would surely have been in a stronger spiritual condition when tempted to deny his Lord.

A BIBLE VERSE EACH DAY

Elijah was a human being, even as we are. He prayed earnestly that it would not rain, and it did not rain on the land for three and a half years.

— James 5: 17 NIV

Elijah had work to do for God in Cherith. Unseen, fervent, praying work. Such work can only be done in the secret place of the Most High. *'He that dwelleth in the secret place of the most High shall abide under the shadow of the Almighty.'* (Psalm 91:1 KJV)

Praise, Thanksgiving and Thankfulness

PORTIONS WERE SERVED TO THEM FROM JOSEPH'S TABLE.

— Genesis 43:34 NIV

The Hebrew word 'portions' is the word *maseth*. It can mean a gift or an oblation and is derived from *nasa'* to lift or carry. When we keep the Remembrance of our Lord Jesus, it is our privilege to lift up our tribute of praise and thanksgiving for the One who did all God's will. As the Levites bore the ark on their shoulders, so we lift up the name of Jesus.

A BIBLE VERSE EACH DAY

Then Moses and the Israelites sang this song to the Lord: 'I will sing to the Lord, for he is highly exalted. ... He has become my salvation. He is my God, and I will praise him, my father's God, and I will exalt him.

— Exodus 15:1,2 NIV

The anthem of praise that burst from full hearts that day, was written by Moses the man of God. He gave voice to the wave of thankfulness that swept through the congregation of Israel. Heartfelt singing is of central importance to God's worshipping people.

'The Lord be with you!' 'The Lord bless you!' they answered.

— Ruth 2:4 NIV

Thus Boaz, Ruth's redeemer, greeted the reapers when he came from Bethlehem. Our redeemer, also came to us from Bethlehem. 'Immanuel - God with us'. Boaz's words to the reapers take on an added significance and our hearts reply: 'The Lord Bless you!'

> *'We bless and praise Thee gracious God*
> *For giving Thine own Son,*
> *Who did partake of flesh and blood,*
> *In all our sorrows one'* (PHSS no. 5)

— *C.M. Luxmoore*

Praise, Thanksgiving and Thankfulness

> Hezekiah gave the order to sacrifice the burnt offering on the altar. As the offering began, singing to the LORD began also.
>
> — 2 Chronicles 29:27 NIV

Singing God's praise was, and always will be, an integral part of the worship and the service of God. *'Outside the inner gate were the chambers for the singers in the inner court.'* (Ezekiel 40:44 NKJV). Something vital is missing when the voice of praise is silent, or is silenced.

> Sing the praises of the Lord, you his faithful people; praise his holy name...You turned my wailing into dancing; you removed my sackcloth and clothed me with joy, that my heart may sing your praises and not be silent. Lord my God, I will praise you forever.
>
> — Psalm 30:4,11,12 NIV

In our praise, we remember that our joy was bought with a price that goes far beyond human measure because our Redeemer was and is the eternal Son of God. As Son of Man, He embodied all the fulness and perfection of the Eternal, Almighty, Holy God who made heaven and earth, yet He died for us.

The Priesthood of Christ

Unity...like precious oil...running down on the beard...on Aaron's beard.

— Psalm 133:2 NIV

The holy anointing oil was reserved for the consecration of Aaron and his sons to priesthood service.

Their ministry foreshadowed that of the Lord Jesus in his high priestly activity on behalf of his people individually and collectively: as our Advocate with the Father at the throne of grace (Heb 4:16) and as 'Great Priest over the House of God' (Heb 10:21). The fragrance of our High Priest delights the heart of God.

Human Pride

BUT WHEN HIS HEART BECAME ARROGANT AND HARDENED WITH PRIDE, HE WAS DEPOSED FROM HIS ROYAL THRONE AND STRIPPED OF HIS GLORY.

— DANIEL 5:20 NIV

It has been well said that 'pride goes before a fall'. Daniel reminded King Belshazzar of the judgement that had befallen Nebuchadnezzar which taught him a reverence for God that was lacking in Belshazzar. 'God is not mocked, for whatever one sows, that will he also reap.' (Gal. 6:7 ESV)

A BIBLE VERSE EACH DAY

Jesus said to them, 'It is not the healthy who need a doctor, but the sick. I have not come to call the righteous, but sinners.'

— Mark 2:17 NIV

This goes to the heart of the matter. Only those who honestly admit their guilt before God can expect forgiveness. Those who believe they have no need of forgiveness, place themselves beyond the reach of God's mercy.

The men of Nineveh will rise up in the judgment with this generation and condemn it, for they repented at the preaching of Jonah; and indeed a greater than Jonah is here.

— Luke 11:32 NIV

How much more culpable were those who refused to repent of their sins at the preaching of the Lord Jesus Christ. The greatest barriers to reconciliation and peace with God that any person can erect, are pride and self-righteousness.

Promise

THROUGH YOUR OFFSPRING ALL NATIONS ON EARTH
WILL BE BLESSED, BECAUSE YOU HAVE OBEYED ME.

— Genesis 22:18 NIV

After Abraham died, God renewed this promise to both Isaac and Jacob. Three times over, God promised: *'through your offspring all nations on earth will be blessed.'* From their vantage point in time, Abraham, Isaac and Jacob could not fully appreciate exactly how God would keep that promise: by sending His Son to redeem *'persons from every tribe and language and people and nation...'* (Rev 5:9). How good is the God we adore!

A BIBLE VERSE EACH DAY

Do not be afraid or discouraged because of the king of Assyria and the vast army with him, for there is a greater power with us than with him. With him is only the arm of flesh, but with us is the Lord our God to help us and to fight our battles.

— 2 Chronicles 32:7,8 NIV

'The soul that on Jesus has leaned for repose,
I will not, I cannot desert to its foes,
That soul though all hell should endeavour to shake,
I'll never, no never, no never forsake.'

— R. Keen, 1785 (PHSS 194)

The word of the Lord came to me: 'What do you see, Jeremiah?' 'I see the branch of an almond tree,' I replied. The Lord said to me, 'You have seen correctly, for I am watching to see that my word is fulfilled.'

— Jeremiah 1:11,12 NIV

This is visionary. Jeremiah saw an almond tree, in Hebrew a 'watcher' tree, a tree that bursts into life at the first sign of Spring. The LORD showed Jeremiah that He actively watches over His promises to bring them to fruition. 'The Lord is not slack concerning his promise...' (2 Pet 3:9)

Promise

> But you, Bethlehem, in the land of Judah, are by no means least among the rulers of Judah; for out of you will come a ruler who will shepherd my people Israel.
>
> — Matthew 2:6 NIV

When the Magi asked Herod where the king of the Jews would be born, the chief priests and teachers of the law found the answer in Micah chapter 5. That prophetic passage goes on to describe His origin thus: 'whose goings forth are from of old, from everlasting.' (Micah 5:2 NKJV)

> The promises were spoken to Abraham and to his seed...meaning one person, who is Christ...if the inheritance depends on the law, then it no longer depends on the promise
>
> — Galatians 3:16,18 NIV

The enactment and culmination of the promise, was not the giving of the law at Sinai. It was enacted at Calvary when our Saviour died to free us from sin. It culminated in the sanctification of a worshipping people in Churches of God: *'a spiritual house', 'a holy temple in the Lord; ... a habitation of God in the Spirit.'* (1 Pet. 2:5; Eph 2:21,22)

Divine Providence

THE LORD WAS WITH JOSEPH SO THAT HE PROS-
PERED...AND GAVE HIM SUCCESS IN WHATEVER
HE DID.

— GEN 39:2,23 NIV

Whether he was sold as a slave or wrongfully accused and jailed, the LORD was with Joseph in all his trials. Through him, Israel would be saved from famine and ultimately redeemed out of Egypt; they would become a Holy Nation and build a sanctuary for God to dwell among them. 'he sent a man before them...' (Ps 105:17) God has done the same for us and more, in the person of His Son!

Then he cried out to the LORD, and the LORD showed him a tree; and he threw it into the waters, and the waters became sweet.

— Exodus 15:25 NASB

The Lord has shown us a tree too - the cursèd tree on which our Lord was crucified. It is that tree alone that makes the bitter sweet, when we bring the One who died on the tree into the experience with us.

As it turned out, she was working in a field belonging to Boaz.

— Ruth 2:3 NIV

Ruth just happened to come across this field, she had no idea whose it was, a completely random choice on her part. But the unseen hand of God was working, guiding her into position for unimagined blessing.

> 'WOULD YOU BRING ME A LITTLE WATER IN A JAR..?'
> AS SHE WAS GOING TO GET IT, HE CALLED, 'AND
> BRING ME, PLEASE, A PIECE OF BREAD.'...SHE
> REPLIED, 'I DON'T HAVE ANY BREAD.'
>
> — 1 KINGS 17:10-12 NIV

We almost feel her heart sinking. This was the last straw. She was forced to reveal her dire poverty. Sometimes we hide the true state of our hearts from each other. But we cannot hide it from God. As soon as she acknowledged her need, God gave her a wonderful promise: *'The jar of flour will not be used up and the jug of oil will not run dry.'*

> EVEN IF I WASHED MYSELF WITH SOAP...YOU WOULD
> PLUNGE ME INTO A SLIME PIT...HE IS NOT A MERE
> MORTAL LIKE ME...IF ONLY THERE WERE SOMEONE
> TO MEDIATE BETWEEN US, SOMEONE TO BRING US
> TOGETHER.
>
> — JOB 9:30-33 NIV

Job was acutely aware that he needed someone to effect a reconciliation between himself and God. No matter how hard we may try to change our behaviour, we cannot wash away our sinful nature and make ourselves righteous before God. Only Jesus can do that for us: *'For there is one God and one mediator between God and mankind, the man Christ Jesus.'* (1 Tim. 2:5)

A BIBLE VERSE EACH DAY

If only there were someone to mediate between us, someone to bring us together, someone to remove God's rod from me.

— Job 9:33,34 NIV

Being children of Adam, we inherit original sin; like a tree whose heartwood is damaged beyond repair our days are numbered. We needed an adjudicator, a mediator, someone with the ability to 'lay his hand upon us both' and reconcile us to God. Jesus came to give us a new heart! We are saved 'through the washing of rebirth and renewal by the Holy Spirit' (Titus 3:5)

⁓

Lift up your eyes and look to the heavens: Who created all these? He who brings out the starry host one by one and calls forth each of them by name. Because of his great power and mighty strength, not one of them is missing.

— Isaiah 40:26 NIV

The Lord Jesus told His disciples that they were of more value than many sparrows and that the hairs of their head were all accounted for. Does not He who 'made the stars', also care for those who put their trust in Him? 'Happy are the people whose God is the Lord!' (Ps. 144:15 NKJV)

⁓

Divine Providence

I SEE FOUR MEN WALKING AROUND IN THE FIRE, UNBOUND AND UNHARMED, AND THE FOURTH LOOKS LIKE A SON OF THE GODS.

— Daniel 3:25 NIV

Time and again God has promised to bless those who obey His word: *'When you walk through the fire, you will not be burned; the flames will not set you ablaze. For I am the Lord your God, the Holy One of Israel, your Saviour.'* (Is. 43:2,3 NIV)

'Those who honour me I will honour.' (1 Sam. 2:30 NIV)

'HOW MANY LOAVES DO YOU HAVE?' THEY SAID, 'SEVEN, AND A FEW SMALL FISH.'...AND THEY ALL ATE AND WERE SATISFIED. AND THEY TOOK UP SEVEN BASKETS FULL OF THE BROKEN PIECES LEFT OVER. THOSE WHO ATE WERE FOUR THOUSAND MEN, BESIDES WOMEN AND CHILDREN.

— Matthew 15:34-38 NIV

Four thousand men PLUS women and children, fed, filled and satisfied from seven loaves and a few small fish! AND - seven baskets FULL of leftovers! The Lord whom we serve is able to take the meagre offerings that we bring and multiply them until they provide such a super-abundance that they meet *'our needs and more'*!

A BIBLE VERSE EACH DAY

'Tell me, what do you have in the house?' 'Nothing at all, except a flask of olive oil,' she replied ... Her sons kept bringing jars to her, and she filled one after another. Soon every container was full to the brim! 'Bring me another jar,' she said to one of her sons.'There aren't any more!' he told her. And then the olive oil stopped flowing. When she told the man of God what had happened, he said to her, 'Now sell the olive oil and pay your debts, and you and your sons can live on what is left over.'

— 2 Kings 4:5-7 NLT

'If I have but Jesus, only Jesus,
Nothing else in all the world beside—
O then everything is mine in Jesus;
For my needs and more He will provide.'

— Anna Ölander, 1861-1939

'God shall fulfill every need of yours according to his riches in glory in Christ Jesus.' (Philippians 4:19 RV)

The Purposes of God

As they were gathering in Galilee, Jesus said to them, 'The Son of Man is about to be delivered into the hands of men, and they will kill him, and he will be raised on the third day.'

— Matthew 17:22,23 ESV

In the foreknowledge of God, the Lord Jesus was following a predetermined plan. Both Jew and Gentile are guilty of the greatest injustice ever carried out, yet God in sovereign mercy forgives and redeems all who put their trust in the risen Saviour. That's divine love in action.

'HIS NAME IS JOHN.' IMMEDIATELY HIS MOUTH WAS OPENED ... AND HE BEGAN TO SPEAK, PRAISING GOD ... 'AND YOU, MY CHILD, WILL BE CALLED A PROPHET OF THE MOST HIGH; FOR YOU WILL GO ON BEFORE THE LORD TO PREPARE THE WAY FOR HIM.'

— LUKE 1:63-76 NIV

Zechariah and Elisabeth, both well on in years, were spared the anguish of hearing how their only son John was murdered by Herod. That would have been too much for them to bear. In the wisdom of God, John was born at the end of their life together, not at the beginning.

IN THE FIFTEENTH YEAR OF THE REIGN OF TIBERIUS CAESAR - WHEN PONTIUS PILATE WAS GOVERNOR OF JUDEA, HEROD TETRARCH OF GALILEE, HIS BROTHER PHILIP TETRARCH OF ITUREA AND TRACONITIS, AND LYSANIAS TETRARCH OF ABILENE - DURING THE HIGH-PRIESTHOOD OF ANNAS AND CAIAPHAS, THE WORD OF GOD CAME TO JOHN SON OF ZECHARIAH IN THE WILDERNESS.

— LUKE 3:1,2 NIV

God had an exact time for John to begin his unique wilderness ministry. The word of God came to him with such power that thousands repented and were baptised in readiness for the appearance of their long awaited Messiah. God is never too late, never too early, always on time.

The Purposes of God

> Did not the Messiah have to suffer these things and then enter his glory?
>
> — Luke 24:26 NIV

The resurrection was no 'spur of the moment' decision by Almighty God. It was planned before the dawn of time, because our omniscient (all knowing) God knows the end from the beginning; He is in complete control; and whatever men or demons or Satan may say or do to contradict or obstruct, they can never thwart the purposes of God. What He has decreed will be fulfilled!

> You do not support the root, but the root supports you.
>
> — Romans 11:18 NIV

Paul said the Roman believers obtained mercy because, in rejecting Christ, Israel abandoned the original purpose to which God called their ancestors. Gentile believers must not think they are any better than the Jews because, in God's purposes of grace, Christ is going to come and deliver His ancient people. 'In this way all Israel will be saved' (v. 26). Praise God! 'How unsearchable his judgments, and his paths beyond tracing out!' (v. 33)

His intent was that now, through the church, the manifold wisdom of God should be made known to the rulers and authorities in the heavenly realms, according to his eternal purpose that he accomplished in Christ Jesus our Lord.

— Eph. 3:10,11 NIV

The *'eternal purpose'* of God involved the uniting of Jew and Gentile, not only in the church which is His body, but in *'a spiritual house', 'a holy temple in the Lord', 'a habitation of God in the Spirit'* (Eph 2:19-22) All this will have a more glorious expression in our eternal home.

Reconciliation

THE SOLDIERS ... CLOTHED HIM WITH PURPLE ... TWISTED A CROWN OF THORNS, PUT IT ON HIS HEAD, AND BEGAN TO SALUTE HIM, 'HAIL, KING OF THE JEWS!' ... THEY STRUCK HIM ON THE HEAD WITH A REED AND SPAT ON HIM; AND BOWING THE KNEE, THEY WORSHIPPED HIM.

— MARK 15:16-19 NKJV

The Gentiles, represented by the Roman soldiers, are as guilty as the Jews, of despising and rejecting their Saviour. Despite this, how grateful we should be that 'God was reconciling the world to himself in Christ, not counting people's sins against them' (2 Cor. 5:19 NIV)

> Why not just accept the injustice and leave it at that? Why not let yourselves be cheated?
>
> — 1 Corinthians 6:7 NLT

Paul puts this searching question to those in the church who were taking each other to court instead of dealing with the matter internally. Disciples of Christ should be better than that, because we follow the One who *'did not retaliate when he was insulted, nor threaten revenge when he suffered. He left his case in the hands of God, who always judges fairly.'* (1 Pet. 2:23 NLT)

Redemption

I WILL DELIVER THIS PEOPLE FROM THE POWER OF THE GRAVE; I WILL REDEEM THEM FROM DEATH. WHERE, O DEATH, ARE YOUR PLAGUES? WHERE, O GRAVE, IS YOUR DESTRUCTION?

— HOSEA 13:14 NIV

'Where, O death, is your victory? Where, O death, is your sting?' The sting of death is sin, and the power of sin is the law. But thanks be to God! He gives us the victory through our Lord Jesus Christ.' (1 Cor. 15:55-57 NIV)

A BIBLE VERSE EACH DAY

John saw Jesus coming toward him and said, 'Look, the Lamb of God, who takes away the sin of the world!'

— John 1:29 NIV

What a momentous thing it was that our Saviour accomplished. On the cross, He took away, not just our individual sins, but the sin of the world. With the exception of unbelief and blasphemy against the Holy Spirit, He has cleared away every obstacle to God's forgiveness.

> *'He hell in hell laid low,*
> *Made sin, He sin o'erthrew,*
> *Bowed to the grave, destroyed it so,*
> *And death by dying slew.'*
>
> — S.W. Gandy 1780-1851
> (PHSS 45)

Redemption

AS A LAMB THAT IS LED TO THE SLAUGHTER, AND AS A SHEEP THAT BEFORE HER SHEARERS IS DUMB; YES, HE OPENED NOT HIS MOUTH. BY OPPRESSION AND JUDGMENT HE WAS TAKEN AWAY; AND AS FOR HIS GENERATION, WHO AMONG THEM CONSIDERED THAT HE WAS CUT OFF OUT OF THE LAND OF THE LIVING?

— ISAIAH 53:7-8

A lamb *'led to the slaughter"*. Innocent and pure. A lamb is helpless, weak in comparison with the strength of a man. The Lord Jesus Christ was not weak: He could have destroyed those miserable men in a moment; but a lamb is SUBMISSIVE - He submitted himself to their cruelty and injustice because He had submitted Himself to the will of God and the work of redemption God had given Him. He had come to make atonement for all mankind by the sacrifice of Himself.

'As a sheep before her shearers is dumb' - he did not defend Himself, though innocent of all charges. Only the Son of the Most High could have accomplished such a work of divine Grace. Only the unique vision of the eternal Son of God could see beyond the abuse He was subjected to by men; see beyond the crushing load of sin He bore on Calvary's cross and *'see of the travail of his soul and be satisfied'*. Beyond untold suffering, He saw the myriads of the redeemed who will praise His name for all eternity. In the remembrance feast which we keep, His words are full of meaning: *'this is my body ... given FOR YOU'* - *'this is the new covenant in my blood which is poured out FOR YOU.'*

Repentance

THIS IS WHAT THE SOVEREIGN LORD, THE HOLY ONE OF ISRAEL, SAYS: 'IN REPENTANCE AND REST IS YOUR SALVATION, IN QUIETNESS AND TRUST IS YOUR STRENGTH, BUT YOU WOULD HAVE NONE OF IT.

— ISAIAH 30:15 NIV

These words are reiterated by the prophet Ezekiel: 'Turn! Turn from your evil ways! Why will you die...?' (Ezek.33:11) True and lasting peace is found when we turn away from self and sin and rest in the Word of God. Jesus said 'I will give you rest' (Mat. 11:28). How sad that so many reject His overtures of love.

SEEK THE LORD WHILE HE MAY BE FOUND; CALL ON HIM WHILE HE IS NEAR. LET THE WICKED FORSAKE THEIR WAYS AND THE UNRIGHTEOUS THEIR THOUGHTS. LET THEM TURN TO THE LORD, AND HE WILL HAVE MERCY ON THEM, AND TO OUR GOD, FOR HE WILL FREELY PARDON.

— ISAIAH 55:6,7 NIV

This suggests that there is a time to respond to the voice of God; that it is possible for a person to resist the voice of God until God gives them up. This is too awful to contemplate. *'now is the time of God's favour, now is the day of salvation.'* (2 Cor 6:2 NIV) We may infer from the little word 'while', that the Lord will not always be so easily reached. The time to turn from self and sin, is while the still, small voice of God's Holy Spirit is speaking to our heart, calling us to seek God's forgiveness.

∾

COME, AND LET US RETURN TO THE LORD; FOR HE HAS TORN, BUT HE WILL HEAL US; HE HAS STRICKEN, BUT HE WILL BIND US UP.

— HOSEA 6:1 NKJV

Our Father in heaven only wants what's best for us. Sometimes we go our own way, like wayward sheep. 'The Shepherd and Guardian of our souls' may then have to teach us some hard lessons, so that we return to Him in our hearts.

∾

Repentance

Take words with you and return to the Lord. Say to him:' Forgive all our sins and receive us graciously, that we may offer the fruit of our lips.'

— Hosea 14:2 NIV

When we acknowledge our failures and ask God to forgive us, He will receive us with open arms, just as in Luke 15, the father welcomed his lost son. ''I will heal their waywardness and love them freely, for my anger has turned away from them.' (Hosea 14:4)

Rend your heart and not your garments. Return to the Lord your God, for he is gracious and compassionate, slow to anger and abounding in love.

— Joel 2:13 NIV

Many mistakenly think that God rewards good deeds, regardless of whether they've had a deep-seated change of heart. This verse tells us that a superficial cleaning up of the outside of the house won't do; God's purpose is nothing less than the complete renewal of our heart and mind.

WHEN GOD SAW WHAT THEY DID AND HOW THEY TURNED FROM THEIR EVIL WAYS, HE RELENTED AND DID NOT BRING ON THEM THE DESTRUCTION HE HAD THREATENED.

— JONAH 3:10 NIV

No-one is 'predestined' to a lost eternity. The purpose of Jonah's preaching was to give the people of Nineveh an opportunity to repent, to turn from their evil ways and seek God's mercy and forgiveness. If their behaviour made no difference to God's response, then Jonah's preaching was futile.

AND I WILL POUR ON THE HOUSE OF DAVID AND ON THE INHABITANTS OF JERUSALEM THE SPIRIT OF GRACE AND SUPPLICATION; THEN THEY WILL LOOK ON ME WHOM THEY PIERCED. YES, THEY WILL MOURN FOR HIM AS ONE MOURNS FOR HIS ONLY SON.

— ZECHARIAH 12:10 NKJV

When the remnant of Israel see their nail-pierced Messiah, their pride will evaporate. The Spirit of God will bring about a godly sorrow. To a man, the nation of Israel will accept Him as their Saviour. 'To him be the glory forever!' (Rom. 11:36 NIV)

Repentance

> Produce fruit in keeping with repentance...The ax is already at the root of the trees, and every tree that does not produce good fruit will be cut down and thrown into the fire.
>
> — Matthew 3:8-10 NIV

Genuine repentance for sin always results in the good fruit of changed behaviour. Fake repentance talks a good game but the behaviour doesn't change. God is the divine woodcutter. Those who refuse to turn from their sin will be permanently cut down and destroyed.

> Those eighteen who died when the tower in Siloam fell on them—do you think they were more guilty ... No! But unless you repent, you too will all perish.
>
> — Luke 13:4,5 NIV

Natural and man-made disasters happen because we live in a fallen world. The Lord Jesus reminded us that as sinners, we are heading for eternal destruction unless we repent and turn to Him.

A BIBLE VERSE EACH DAY

IN THE SAME WAY, I TELL YOU, THERE IS REJOICING IN THE PRESENCE OF THE ANGELS OF GOD OVER ONE SINNER WHO REPENTS.

— LUKE 15:10 NIV

In Luke 15, the Lord Jesus illustrates the preciousness of a lost sheep to a shepherd; of a high value coin to a woman who swept diligently until she found it; of a lost son to a father and of a lost soul to God.

I HAVE DECLARED TO BOTH JEWS AND GREEKS THAT THEY MUST TURN TO GOD IN REPENTANCE AND HAVE FAITH IN OUR LORD JESUS.

— ACTS 20:21 NIV

Paul and the apostles emphatically proclaimed the fundamental change that had to take place so that a person would be saved. Before God, they had to turn away from the morally and spiritually bankrupt way of life and put their trust in Jesus as their Saviour and their Lord.

Reward

WHEN DAVID REACHED ZIKLAG, HE SENT SOME OF THE PLUNDER TO THE ELDERS OF JUDAH, WHO WERE HIS FRIENDS, SAYING, 'HERE IS A GIFT FOR YOU FROM THE PLUNDER OF THE LORD'S ENEMIES.'

— 1 SAMUEL 30:26 NIV

David was generous in rewarding those who had shown him friendship. He did not forget them. The Lord Jesus promised great reward to those who remain faithful to Him (Luke 22:29).

'Those who trust Him wholly,
Find Him wholly true.'

— F.R. HAVERGAL

A BIBLE VERSE EACH DAY

For God is not unjust so as to overlook your work and the love that you have shown for his name in serving the saints, as you still do.

— Hebrews 6:10 ESV

God took note of the work of those Hebrew Christians of a past day to whom the apostle was writing. He has taken note of the work of every disciple who attempts anything for God's glory. *'he will reward each person according to what they have done.'* (Matthew 16:27)

∿

I saw the souls of them that had been beheaded for the testimony of Jesus, and for the word of God, and such as worshipped not the beast, neither his image, and received not the mark upon their forehead and upon their hand; and they lived, and reigned with Christ a thousand years.

— Revelation 20:4 RV

What a reward! They were faithful unto death; They will reign with Christ and administer his upright and beneficial policies for a thousand years. Instead of enduring hell on earth, they will enjoy heaven on earth.

∿

Reward

> The one who is victorious I will make a pillar in the temple of my God. Never again will they leave it. I will write on them the name of my God and the name of the city of my God, the new Jerusalem ... and I will also write on them my new name.
>
> — Revelation 3:12 NIV

What a star studded reward! To be a permanent pillar in the temple of God; to have the name of God written on us; plus the name of the new Jerusalem; plus the new name of our risen Lord! Such honours will be held in high esteem forever and ever.

> with your blood you purchased for God persons from every ... nation. You have made them to be a kingdom and priests to serve our God, and they will reign on the earth.
>
> — Revelation 5:9,10 NIV

A kingdom denotes a king and those who obey his rule. Priests serve in God's house and present Him with sacrifices of appreciation and thanksgiving. Such will have the privilege of reigning upon the earth. *'He that overcomes, I will give to him to sit down with me in my throne'* (Revelation 3:21)

A BIBLE VERSE EACH DAY

'Behold, I come quickly; and my reward is with me, to render to each man according as his work is.'

— Revelation 22:12

This for the disciple of Christ, is the 'antidote' to the feeling of despondency king Solomon had as he contemplated the inevitability of the day of death and the consequent futility of all human endeavour. He concluded: *'all is vanity and a striving after wind'* (Eccles. 2:17). On the contrary, the promise of future reward from the Lord Jesus gives eternal significance to every aspect of our lives on earth. *'whatsoever you do, in word or in deed, do all in the name of the Lord Jesus' (Col. 3:17)* - this is the spirit in which we should view every task, no matter how trivial or mundane. If we do it in HIS NAME, then the day will come when He says to us *'Well done good and faithful servant, enter you into the joy of your Lord'.* Such service, which many despise as trivial, menial, ephemeral down here, in that day, will be shown to have been highly valued by Him. Then it will be very clear that all we did from a desire to bring glory to God, had an eternal significance: for those who have been *'lights in a dark place'*, reflecting His glory and His grace to those around us, will receive an eternal reward for their work.

> *The trivial round, the common task,*
> *Will furnish all we need to ask;*
> *Room to deny ourselves, a road*
> *To bring us daily nearer God.*
>
> — J. Keble, 1792-1866
> (PHSS 492)

Resurrection

WHEN YOU ENTER THE LAND...AND YOU REAP ITS HARVEST, BRING TO THE PRIEST A SHEAF OF THE FIRST GRAIN YOU HARVEST. HE IS TO WAVE THE SHEAF BEFORE THE LORD SO IT WILL BE ACCEPTED ON YOUR BEHALF; THE PRIEST IS TO WAVE IT ON THE DAY AFTER THE SABBATH.

— LEVITICUS 23:NIV

The sheaf of the firstfruits is a picture of Christ in resurrection. The priest waved it before God on the first day of the week, the day after the Sabbath - on resurrection morning! *'Christ, the firstfruits; then, when he comes, those who belong to him.'* (1 Cor. 15:23)

> Have pity on me ... for the hand of God has struck me ... I know that my redeemer lives, and that in the end he will stand on the earth ...yet in my flesh I will see God; I myself will see him with my own eyes - I, and not another.
>
> — Job 19:21-27 NIV

Humanly speaking Job was at his lowest ebb: despised by men, brought low by God, he saw no way out. Paradoxically however, Job had reached a spiritual high point. God opened the eyes of his heart and by faith he saw and laid hold on the awesome truth of God's future redemptive purposes.

∼

> Why do you look for the living among the dead?
>
> — Luke 24:5 NIV

The Living Christ is not to be found in dead ceremonials, rituals, works of self righteousness, or the processions of empty religion. Look to the risen Lord! He 'has the keys of death and of Hades', He alone has power to give eternal life, to take away the emptiness of a Godless life, because 'He is risen!' He is 'alive forevermore!' (Rev 1:18)

∼

Resurrection

> Look at my hands and my feet. It is I myself! Touch me and see; a ghost does not have flesh and bones, as you see I have.
>
> — Luke 24:39 NIV

The bodily resurrection of Christ is essential to our present and eternal salvation because: *"if Christ has not been raised, your faith is futile; you are still in your sins."* (1 Cor 15:17 NIV) Our redemption depends on the Lord Jesus being raised for our justification just as much as it depends on His death on the cross for our sins.

> I am the resurrection and the life. Whoever believes in me, though he die, yet shall he live.
>
> — John 11:25 ESV

Christ never preached any funeral sermons! To the widow of Nain He said 'Don't Cry' and by Divine power raised her son from the dead. To Martha He said 'Your brother will rise again.' To those who trust Him the Word of God says: 'He will wipe away every tear from their eyes, and death shall be no more' (Rev 21:4)

A BIBLE VERSE EACH DAY

God...has set a day when he will judge the world with justice by the man he has appointed. He has given proof of this to everyone by raising him from the dead.

— Acts 17:30,31 NIV

The resurrection of Jesus Christ is the litmus test for all false religions. No-one else ever rose from the dead. Christ Jesus the man, was able to die and live again. He overcame death. He is alive now; He lives forever. He will never die again. He imparts victory over death and everlasting life to all who accept Him as their Saviour.

∽

But Christ has indeed been raised from the dead, the firstfruits of those who have fallen asleep.

— 1 Corinthians 15:20 NIV

The Lord Jesus Christ is the forerunner of the great harvest of redeemed souls that will be raised from the dead when He returns to the air and calls both the dead in Christ and living believers to Himself. All due to His victory over death on that wonderful first resurrection morning!

∽

Restoration

I WILL GIVE THEM AN UNDIVIDED HEART AND PUT A NEW SPIRIT IN THEM; I WILL REMOVE FROM THEM THEIR HEART OF STONE AND GIVE THEM A HEART OF FLESH. THEN THEY WILL FOLLOW MY DECREES AND BE CAREFUL TO KEEP MY LAWS. THEY WILL BE MY PEOPLE, AND I WILL BE THEIR GOD.

— EZEKIEL 11:19,20 NIV

These words, given to the prophet Ezekiel in Babylon, promised future restoration for the exiles to the land of Israel. A new spirit would cause them to obey His Word with heart and soul. When that happens, God can truly own His people.

And he said to them, 'Is it lawful on the Sabbath to do good or to do harm, to save life or to kill?' But they were silent. And he looked around at them with anger, grieved at their hardness of heart, and said to the man, 'Stretch out your hand.' He stretched it out, and his hand was restored.

— Mark 3:4,5 ESV

No wonder the Lord Jesus was angry with those who were so hard-hearted, they would rather have thwarted his power to heal than see a man whose hand was withered, restored to play a full and useful part in his community. How good to know that our Lord is more than able to overrule those who stand against Him—and also stands ready to transform the lives of those whose potential has been damaged because of sin in the human bloodstream.

Righteousness

The Lord rewards everyone for their righteousness and faithfulness.

— 1 Samuel 26:23 NIV

The divine principle which David alluded to here, when for the second time he had refused to take the life of Saul, God's anointed king, is summed up in the words of the Lord Jesus: 'Do to others as you would have them do to you.' (Luke 6:31 NIV)

> In the land of Uz there lived a man whose name was Job. This man was blameless and upright; he feared God and shunned evil.
>
> — Job 1:1 NIV

In today's money, Job was a millionaire. Yet when his family indulged their appetite for sensual pleasures, Job's intercessory offerings testified to his spiritual integrity. He reflected the work of the Lord Jesus, who is our 'advocate with the Father' (1 Jn 2:1) and of the Holy Spirit, who 'intercedes for us through wordless groans' (Rom 8:26). No wonder God held up Job as an outstanding example of faithful and righteous living!

> Those who are wise will shine like the brightness of the heavens, and those who lead many to righteousness, like the stars for ever and ever.
>
> — Daniel 12:3 NIV

'Those who are wise' means those whose wisdom is based on the eternal truths of the Word of God. 'Those who lead many to righteousness' are those who guide others to trust in the righteousness of Christ rather than their own righteousness. Such persons will be honoured throughout all eternity.

Righteousness

UNLESS YOUR RIGHTEOUSNESS SURPASSES THAT OF THE PHARISEES AND THE TEACHERS OF THE LAW, YOU WILL CERTAINLY NOT ENTER THE KINGDOM OF HEAVEN.

— MATTHEW 5:20 NIV

How can our righteousness exceed that of the scribes and Pharisees who observed in obsessive detail the letter of the law? In the foregoing passage, the Lord emphasises the importance of keeping God's good laws and of their enduring value to Him. The answer is that our righteousness comes not from our own efforts but from Christ's perfect righteousness. In Christ alone we trust as we 'let our light shine before men'. (Matt 5:16)

FOR IN THE GOSPEL THE RIGHTEOUSNESS OF GOD IS REVEALED--A RIGHTEOUSNESS THAT IS BY FAITH FROM FIRST TO LAST, JUST AS IT IS WRITTEN: 'THE RIGHTEOUS WILL LIVE BY FAITH.'

— ROM. 1:17 NIV

Faith in Jesus, 'the Righteous One' (Acts 3:14), is the key to righteousness before God. Self righteousness is like a whitewashed tomb. We need to clothe ourselves in the complete perfection of the One who took all our sins upon Himself. Only in Christ, can dead people live.

> BE CAREFUL TO DO WHAT IS RIGHT IN THE EYES OF EVERYONE. IF IT IS POSSIBLE, AS FAR AS IT DEPENDS ON YOU, LIVE AT PEACE WITH EVERYONE.
>
> — ROMANS 12:17,18 NIV

The example we set affects others. But, 'doing the right thing' must agree with what is right in God's eyes. Regrettably, some think the majority view must prevail even when it contradicts the word of God. At such times, we do what we can to promote friendly relationships without compromising truth and righteousness.

> BY FAITH NOAH...BUILT AN ARK TO SAVE HIS FAMILY. BY HIS FAITH HE CONDEMNED THE WORLD AND BECAME HEIR OF THE RIGHTEOUSNESS THAT IS IN KEEPING WITH FAITH.
>
> — HEBREWS 11:7 NIV

Noah was motivated by reverence for God. He believed God's forewarning. His faith led to actions that were inexplicable to those who did not believe God. Like Abraham, Noah was accounted righteous by God, not because of his own intrinsic goodness but because of his faith in the unfailing truth of the word of God.

Righteousness

> The Sabbath was made for man, not man for the Sabbath.
>
> — Mark 2:27 NIV

When the Pharisees found fault with the disciples for plucking ears of corn on the Sabbath day, 'the Lord of the Sabbath' reminded them that the original purpose of the Sabbath was for man's wellbeing as a day of rest; instead of obsessing about the letter of the law, their focus ought to have been on the benefit to their souls of having a day free for the things of God, unhindered by weekday cares.

The Rock of Ages

OUR FATHERS ... ALL ATE THE SAME SPIRITUAL FOOD, AND ALL DRANK THE SAME SPIRITUAL DRINK. FOR THEY DRANK FROM THE SPIRITUAL ROCK THAT FOLLOWED THEM, AND THE ROCK WAS CHRIST.

— 1 CORINTHIANS 10:1-4 ESV

The rock was *Christ*! These are startling words! Israel's Messiah, our Saviour, The Lord Jesus Christ, was 'the rock' who in pre -incarnation glory, followed them and sustained them spiritually on their journey to the promised land. Today, we also eat and drink of Christ *'our shadowing Rock'* as we journey to our home in heaven. *'The LORD lives, and blessed be my rock, and exalted be the God of my salvation!'* (Psalm 18:46).

Personal Sacrifice

THE LORD IS A GOD WHO KNOWS, AND BY HIM DEEDS ARE WEIGHED.

— 1 SAMUEL 2:3 NIV

God weighs up and measures the value of our actions. Some things might cost you very little but cost another person a lot more. On the face of it, the same action; but God who knows 'the thoughts and intents of the heart' will assess the true cost and value of our deeds.

A BIBLE VERSE EACH DAY

For the eyes of the LORD range throughout the earth to strengthen those whose hearts are fully committed to him.

— 2 Chronicles 16:9 NIV

We can only expect the LORD's blessing upon our endeavours if our heart is 'fully committed' to Him. This requires us to be completely at one with His will and His word. We may achieve this through self-examination, honesty and self-sacrifice in our daily walk with God.

∽

'Truly I tell you,' he said, 'this poor widow has put in more than all the others. All these people gave their gifts out of their wealth; but she out of her poverty put in all she had to live on.'

— Luke 21:3,4 NIV

This incident reminds us of the Lord's words to Samuel when the sons of Jesse were brought before him: 'People look at the outward appearance, but the LORD looks at the heart.' (1 Sam. 16:7 NIV) Sacrificial giving is always noticed by the One who gave Himself as a sacrifice for us.

∽

Personal Sacrifice

Christ, who through the eternal Spirit offered himself unblemished to God.

— Hebrews 9:14 NIV

Unblemished on the cross:

Unblemished when all the billows of divine wrath against our sin went over Him;

Unblemished when He cried *'Eli, Eli, Lama Sabacthini'*;

Unblemished when He dismissed His spirit and *'tasted death for every person.'*

ye have been redeemed ... with precious blood, as of a lamb without blemish and without spot, even the blood of Christ' (1 Pet. 1:18-19).

Because Christ was without blemish, God did not allow His body to see corruption. How much God the Father appreciated that fragrant, free-will offering!

> *'Christ, Spotless, offered Thee Himself,*
> *O what a gift divine!*
> *Its fragrant worth no tongue can tell,*
> *...What joy, O God, was Thine!'*
>
> — C.M. Luxmoore, (1858-1922);
> PHSS Hymnbook, no.5

∾

Salvation

ALL THAT NIGHT THE LORD DROVE THE SEA BACK WITH A STRONG EAST WIND AND TURNED IT INTO DRY LAND. THE WATERS WERE DIVIDED, AND THE ISRAELITES WENT THROUGH THE SEA ON DRY GROUND, WITH A WALL OF WATER ON THEIR RIGHT AND ON THEIR LEFT.

— Ex. 14:21,22 NIV

Not only did the LORD save Israel from their enemies, He permanently removed the threat of recapture. God doesn't do things by halves. He is able to *'save to the uttermost'* (Heb. 7:25 RV) all who come to Him through Jesus.

> Yet I am the Lord your God ever since the land of Egypt, and you shall know no God but Me; for there is no saviour besides Me.
>
> — Hosea 13:4 NKJV

Israel turned their backs on God and rejected the only person who could save them from spiritual and eternal death. The God who saved Israel from slavery in Egypt is the same God who sent His Son to be our Saviour. If we turn our backs on Him, we do it to our everlasting destruction.

> Is not this man a burning stick snatched from the fire?
>
> — Zechariah 3:2 NIV

As sinners, we are already condemned. Our only hope of salvation is to cry out to Christ who died for us and rose again. He alone has the power to rescue us from eternal destruction in the lake of fire. (Rev. 21:8)

Salvation

And Jesus said to him, 'Today salvation has come to this house, since he also is a son of Abraham. For the Son of Man came to seek and to save the lost.'

— Luke 19:9,10 ESV

Like Abraham, Zacchaeus became a man of faith. He put his trust in Jesus the Messiah, the Son of God, the Saviour of lost sinners. When his soul was enriched, he discovered 'it is more blessed to give than to receive'.

You turned to God from idols to serve the living and true God, and to wait for his Son from heaven, whom he raised from the dead—Jesus, who rescues us from the coming wrath.

— 1 Thessalonians 1:9,10 NIV

Christianity is not a dead religion. As disciples of Christ, we serve a living God and a risen saviour. Our trust is wholly in Jesus, who took our sins away, and saved us from God's judgement on unrepentant sinners. With growing anticipation, we await His soon return.

HE IS ABLE TO SAVE COMPLETELY THOSE WHO COME TO GOD THROUGH HIM, BECAUSE HE ALWAYS LIVES TO INTERCEDE FOR THEM.

— HEBREWS 7:25 NIV

This full and complete salvation involves far more than salvation from eternal destruction - it involves a lifetime of drawing near to God to enjoy fellowship and communion as we gladly serve Him - and when this life is over, encompasses the vast, unending future blessings that God has in store for us.

HER MOTHER IN LAW...SAID, WHO ART THOU, MY DAUGHTER?

— RUTH 3:16 KJV

Perhaps it was the dim light; or, had such a change come over Ruth that Naomi hardly recognised her? Instead of sorrow and despair, Ruth now carried the promise of a gentleman.

The heart of the sinner who comes to Jesus for mercy can sing:*'What a wonderful change in my life has been wrought, Since Jesus came into my heart!'*—Rufus H. McDaniel (1914)

Christ makes all the difference to those whose who take Him at His word!

Salvation

> I CANNOT REDEEM IT...AND HE REMOVED HIS SANDAL.
>
> — RUTH 4:6,8 NIV

The transaction was sealed by this uncomplicated ancient custom – a shoe handed from one person to another. As if to say, 'its yours now. I give up all rights to it.' Praise God! When the Lord Jesus paid the redemption price for our souls by his death on the cross, Satan had to give up any rights he ever had to claim us as his own.

> GOD HAS DELIVERED ME FROM GOING DOWN TO THE PIT, AND I SHALL LIVE TO ENJOY THE LIGHT OF LIFE.
>
> — JOB 33:28 NIV

It is God who in mercy, rescues people from the consequences of their sin: the awful darkness of a lost eternity in the Lake of Fire. He sent His beloved Son to die so that we could enjoy the light of eternal life. Jesus said: 'he that follows me shall not walk in the darkness, but shall have the light of life.' (John 8:12)

A BIBLE VERSE EACH DAY

HE ... BORE OUR SUFFERING...HE BORE THE SIN OF MANY, AND MADE INTERCESSION FOR THE TRANSGRESSORS.

— Isaiah 53:4,12 NIV

He himself bore our sins' in his body on the cross, so that we might die to sins and live for righteousness; 'by his wounds you have been healed.'

— 1 Peter 2:24 NIV

Ransomed, healed, restored, forgiven,
Who like thee His praise should sing?'

— H.F. Lyte, 1834
(PHSS 165)

May we live our lives in such a way.

SANCTIFICATION

FOLLOW AFTER PEACE WITH ALL MEN, AND THE SANCTIFICATION WITHOUT WHICH NO MAN SHALL SEE THE LORD.

— HEBREWS 12:14 RV

In contrast to ordinary observation, the Greek word 'see', in this verse means 'to gaze ...with wide-open eyes, as at something remarkable' (Strong). It suggests that those who keep themselves *'unspotted from the world'* (Jas 1:27), will discover what David valued so highly: *'that I may dwell in the house of the Lord all the days of my life, to gaze on the beauty of the Lord and to seek him in his temple.'* (Ps 27:4)

Eternal Security

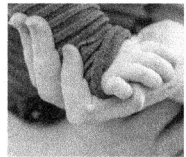

I GIVE THEM ETERNAL LIFE, AND THEY SHALL NEVER PERISH; NO ONE WILL SNATCH THEM OUT OF MY HAND. MY FATHER...IS GREATER THAN ALL; NO ONE CAN SNATCH THEM OUT OF MY FATHER'S HAND.

— JOHN 10:28,29 NIV

Jesus spoke about the real and permanent security that He gives to all who put their trust in Him. This security is spiritual and eternal, therefore nothing can take it away, neither in this world or the next. It's a security we cannot work for and will never lose because it was purchased for us by Jesus sin-atoning death on the cross.

A BIBLE VERSE EACH DAY

My sheep listen to my voice; I know them, and they follow me. I give them eternal life, and they shall never perish; no one will snatch them out of my hand. My Father, who has given them to me, is greater than all; no one can snatch them out of my Father's hand.

— John 10:27-29 NIV

The security of the believer on Jesus is doubly sure: we are held safe in the hands of both the Father and the Son.

> *What from Christ the soul can sever,*
> *Bound by everlasting bands?*
> *Once in Him, in Him for ever,*
> *Thus the eternal covenant stands.*
>
> — John Kent 1766-1843
> (PHSS 117)

SERVICE

SHALL YOUR BROTHERS GO TO THE WAR WHILE YOU SIT HERE?

— NUMBERS 32:6 ESV

Let none hear you idly saying,
'There is nothing I can do,'
While the souls of men are dying,
And the Master calls for you,
Take the task He gives you gladly,
Let His work your pleasure be;
Answer gladly when He calleth -
'Here am I, send me, send me.'

— DANIEL MARCH 1868
(PHSS 364)

~

A BIBLE VERSE EACH DAY

WHOEVER IS FEARFUL AND TREMBLING, LET HIM RETURN HOME.

— JUDGES 7:3 ESV

When Moshe Dayan took over command of the Northern sector of the Israeli army in 1952, he said to his officers: *'Anyone who doesn't want to...is free to get up and leave...I don't ask anyone here to serve in the army against his will.'* At God's instigation, Gideon took the same approach more than 3000 years before. God doesn't want conscripts - only volunteers!

I WILL PRAISE GOD'S NAME IN SONG AND GLORIFY HIM WITH THANKSGIVING. THIS WILL PLEASE THE LORD MORE THAN AN OX, MORE THAN A BULL WITH ITS HORNS AND HOOVES.

— PSALM 69:30,31 NIV

It's not the size of our gift that matters but the size of our appreciation of Him. God looks on the heart.

THE SILENCE OF THE LAMB

THIS MAN SAID, 'I AM ABLE TO DESTROY THE TEMPLE OF GOD, AND TO REBUILD IT IN THREE DAYS." AND THE HIGH PRIEST STOOD UP AND SAID, 'HAVE YOU NO ANSWER …? WHAT IS IT THAT THESE MEN TESTIFY AGAINST YOU?' BUT JESUS REMAINED SILENT.

— MATTHEW 26: 61-63 ESV

There is a time to speak and a time to be silent. When Jesus rode into Jerusalem the disciples cried *'Hosannah!'* He said *'if these were silent, the very stones would cry out'* (Luke 19:40). When falsely accused, He remained silent because He had come to lay down the temple of His body on our behalf and on the third day rise again. We cannot remain silent about that!

Wilful Sin

I, THE LORD YOUR GOD, AM A JEALOUS GOD, PUNISHING THE CHILDREN FOR THE SIN OF THE PARENTS TO THE THIRD AND FOURTH GENERATION OF THOSE WHO HATE ME, BUT SHOWING LOVE TO A THOUSAND GENERATIONS OF THOSE WHO LOVE ME AND KEEP MY COMMANDMENTS.

— EXODUS 20:5,6 NIV

The New Living Translation says 'the entire family is affected' by their parents sin. Those who reject God and show their hatred of Him by rebellious behaviour, affect their children's well-being for several generations. By contrast, how much more blessed are the children of godly parents!

> WITH MANY SUCH PARABLES HE SPOKE THE WORD TO THEM, AS THEY WERE ABLE TO HEAR IT. HE DID NOT SPEAK TO THEM WITHOUT A PARABLE, BUT PRIVATELY TO HIS OWN DISCIPLES HE EXPLAINED EVERYTHING.
>
> — MARK 4:33,34 ESV

At the beginning of His public ministry, the Lord Jesus spoke plainly, with easily understood language, for example, in the 'Sermon on the Mount'. Later on, when Israel's spiritual leaders wilfully refused to believe Him, He continually spoke to them in parables because they were *'ever hearing, but never understanding'* (Is. 6:9). Their wilful sin met with correspondingly severe judgement.

Sowing the Good Seed

Happy are you who sow beside all waters.

— Isaiah 32:20 ESV

Sow beside all waters
Nor sicken at hope deferred;
Let never a soul through thy dumbness
Be lost for want of a word.

— Anon.

Spiritual Food

THERE WAS FOOD EVERY DAY FOR ELIJAH AND FOR THE WOMAN AND HER FAMILY. FOR THE JAR OF FLOUR WAS NOT USED UP AND THE JUG OF OIL DID NOT RUN DRY.

— 1 KINGS 17:15-16 NIV)

A miracle happened every day. Elijah's God was the same God who fed thousands of Israelites with manna for forty years. The same God sent his beloved Son, who fed five thousand with five loaves and two small fishes and said: *'I am the bread of life. Whoever comes to me will never go hungry, and whoever believes in me will never be thirsty.'* (John 6:35 NIV)

A BIBLE VERSE EACH DAY

And he gave them their request; but sent leanness into their soul.

— Psalm 106:15 KJV

What we want and what we need are often two very different things. Israel got what they wanted in the wilderness but it wasn't for their spiritual good. Far better to let go of the things we want but don't need and let the LORD our Shepherd lead us into the green pastures of His will.

~

'The days are coming,' declares the Sovereign Lord, 'when I will send a famine through the land—not a famine of food or a thirst for water, but a famine of hearing the words of the Lord.'

— Amos 8:11 NIV

In response to those who were so greedy of gain that they exploited the poor, the Sovereign LORD withdrew the Spirit-filled ministry of His word. He 'sent leanness into their soul' so that they would learn that *'man does not live on bread alone but on every word that comes from the mouth of the LORD.'* (Deut. 8:3)

~

Spiritual Vision and Spiritual Blindness

THEN THE FAMILY HEADS OF JUDAH AND BENJAMIN, AND THE PRIESTS AND LEVITES - EVERYONE WHOSE HEART GOD HAD MOVED - PREPARED TO GO UP AND BUILD THE HOUSE OF THE LORD IN JERUSALEM.

— EZRA 1:5 NIV

They had caught the vision of a rebuilt temple to which God's exiled people could return. Just as Isaac had to re-dig the wells his father Abraham had dug (Gen 27), so each succeeding generation of God's people have to 'contend earnestly for the faith', to build and maintain the revealed will of God in relation to his dwelling place on earth.

Yes, you know me, and you know where I am from. I am not here on my own authority, but he who sent me is true. You do not know him, but I know him because I am from him and he sent me.

— JOHN 7:28,29 NIV

The Jewish leaders were spiritually blind to the divine origin of the Lord Jesus, because they were spiritually dead. They didn't have a living relationship with God the Father, as Abraham, Moses and David had. That's why they didn't recognise their Messiah.

SPIRITUAL WEALTH

> JUST THEN BOAZ ARRIVED FROM BETHLEHEM AND GREETED THE HARVESTERS, 'THE LORD BE WITH YOU!' 'THE LORD BLESS YOU!' THEY ANSWERED.
>
> — RUTH 2:4 NIV

Boaz, man of substance and wealth, came from Bethlehem, the House of Bread. What a lovely relationship between master and servants! Ruth must have been impressed by this noble man. Our mighty man of wealth came from Bethlehem too. He is 'the living bread' who came down out of Heaven to repair the damaged relationship between man and God.

'Bring me the shawl you are wearing and hold it out.' When she did so, he poured into it six measures of barley and placed the bundle on her.

— Ruth 3:15 NIV

Boaz gave Ruth a generous token of his pledge. The Lord Jesus, our *'kinsman-redeemer'*, has given the Holy Spirit to each believer as 'an earnest', a token, 'of our inheritance'.

The Holy Spirit, Teacher blest,
Who guides us to our heavenly rest,
Makes these poor hearts His dwelling place,
To whisper there, the tale of grace.
We cannot praise Him as we ought,
His love excels our highest thought!

— C. M Luxmoore, 1858-1922
(PHSS 102)

Spiritual Wealth

> THERE IS A MINE FOR SILVER...THEY TUNNEL THROUGH THE ROCK; THEIR EYES SEE ALL ITS TREASURES.
>
> — JOB 28:1-10 NIV)

Job gives a graphic description of the mining industry of his day: but men's industry and ingenuity, discovering the natural wealth of the earth, fail to bring them spiritual riches. Job asks 'But where shall wisdom be found?' Answering his own question he puts his finger on a profound spiritual truth: *'The fear of the Lord - that is wisdom, and to shun evil is understanding'* (Job 28:28).

SUFFERING AND PERSECUTION

WHY HAVE YOU MADE ME YOUR TARGET? ... FOR I WILL SOON LIE DOWN IN THE DUST; YOU WILL SEARCH FOR ME, BUT I WILL BE NO MORE.

— JOB 7:20,21 NIV

While God was silent Job could make no sense of his troubles. If he had known about Christ's sufferings, he might have been able to say what Christian martyr Margaret Wilson said when asked what she thought of her companion tied to a stake in the Solway Firth: *'I see Christ wrestling there; think ye that we are the sufferers? No; it is Christ in us, for he sends none a warfare at their own charges.'* *

---

* From *"Fair Sunshine"* by Jock Purves, p.81. See bibliography for details.

A BIBLE VERSE EACH DAY

> They gather themselves together against the soul of the righteous, and condemn the innocent blood. But the LORD hath been my high tower.
>
> — Psalm 94:21,22 RV

For those whose lives are governed by faith in God and by His word, persecution is nothing new. As Paul reminded Timothy: 'all who desire to live a godly life in Christ Jesus will be persecuted.' (2 Tim 3:12) Our example is the Lord Jesus: *'...being reviled, He did not revile in return; while suffering, He uttered no threats, but kept entrusting Himself to Him who judges righteously.'* (1 Pet 2:23, NASB)

∾

> It was the LORD's will to crush him and cause him to suffer.
>
> — Isaiah 53:10 NIV

The Hebrew word for the LORD's 'will' in some older versions is translated *'it pleased the LORD to bruise him'*. This cannot mean that God enjoyed inflicting untold suffering on His beloved Son. Instead, as Dr Luxmoore's solemn yet beautiful hymn suggests, the atoning death of the Lord Jesus brought unique satisfaction to the heart of God: *'On Him in whom He had delight, The bitter chastening fell'* (C.M. Luxmoore, 1858-1922 PHSS no. 12)

∾

Suffering and Persecution

> Why did I ever come out of the womb to see trouble and sorrow and to end my days in shame?
>
> — Jeremiah 20:18 NIV

> He was despised and rejected by mankind, a man of suffering, and familiar with pain.
>
> — Isaiah 53:3 NIV

Jeremiah might have had cause to ask such a question - but the Lord Jesus knew He was born to suffer and die for our sins. But even though He knew what to expect, that knowledge didn't make His sufferings any less painful.

∽

> Herod... had James, the brother of John, put to death with the sword. When he saw that this met with approval among the Jews, he proceeded to seize Peter also.
>
> — Acts 12:1-3 NIV

James witnessed the transfiguration of the Lord Jesus. He witnessed His agony in the garden. He was one of the Lord's inner circle, yet here in Jerusalem, Herod cruelly takes his life. But James's name will be engraved forever on the foundations of the New Jerusalem. The Lord has future, eternal purposes for James.

∽

A BIBLE VERSE EACH DAY

The chief official gave them new names: to Daniel, the name Belteshazzar; to Hananiah, Shadrach; to Mishael, Meshach; and to Azariah, Abednego.

— Daniel 1:7 NIV

The names of Daniel and his three companions referred in one way or another to the goodness of the living God. The names given them in Babylon, erased those references. Despite the assault on their spiritual identity, Daniel, Hananiah, Mishael and Azariah remained faithful to God. He vindicated their unswerving devotion by a miraculous deliverance from the burning, fiery furnace. What a tremendous example!

~

Then one of the elders answered, saying to me, 'Who are these arrayed in white robes, and where did they come from?' ... 'Sir, you know.' So he said to me, 'These are the ones who come out of the great tribulation.'

— Revelation 7:13-14 NKJV

John saw a vast, white-robed, multi-national multitude, 'standing before the throne and before the Lamb', surrounded by angels, worshipping with heart and soul and voice. On earth they endured hunger, thirst, homelessness; not any more! *'the Lamb ... will shepherd them ... And God will wipe away every tear from their eyes.'* (Rev. 7:17)

~

Suffering and Persecution

> All this is evidence that God's judgment is right, and as a result you will be counted worthy of the kingdom of God, for which you are suffering. God is just: He will pay back trouble to those who trouble you and give relief to you.
>
> — 2 Thessalonians 1:5-7 NIV

Suffering due to persecution very quickly reveals the quality of a person's faith. Those who are faithful to their Lord no matter what happens, are 'counted worthy of the kingdom of God'. God will reward them for their loyalty. He will also punish their enemies.

THE SUFFERING OF CHRIST

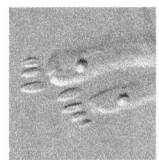

YOU CAST ME INTO THE DEEP, INTO THE HEART OF
THE SEAS, AND THE FLOODS SURROUNDED ME; ALL
YOUR BILLOWS AND YOUR WAVES PASSED OVER ME.

— JONAH 2:3 NKJV)

All the waves and billows of God's wrath descended on His beloved Son at Calvary. He cried out: *'My God, My God, why have you forsaken me?'* There was no deliverance for Him because He was dying to atone for our sins. How grateful we should be for the eternal redemption that He purchased for us with His blood.

A BIBLE VERSE EACH DAY

Do you think I cannot call on my Father, and he will at once put at my disposal more than twelve legions of angels?

— Matthew 26:53 NIV

They bound the hands of Jesus in the garden
   where he prayed
They led him thru the streets in shame
They spat upon the saviour so pure and free
   from sin
They said, 'crucify him: he's to blame.
He could have called ten thousand angels
But he died alone, for you and me.

— Ray Overhalt, 1959

And they laid hands on him and seized him.... And they led Jesus to the high priest.

— Mark 14:46,53 ESV)

We marvel that this mighty One, (in whose holy presence Isaiah, Daniel and John were struck with self-loathing when they were made aware of His glory), was so man-handled and ill treated by men. God permitted it and the Lord submitted Himself to them because He had come to suffer 'yet deeper anguish' on the cross when God *'laid on him the iniquity of us all'* (Isaiah 53).

The Suffering of Christ

THE GOVERNOR'S SOLDIERS ... STRIPPED HIM AND PUT A SCARLET ROBE ON HIM, AND THEN TWISTED TOGETHER A CROWN OF THORNS AND SET IT ON HIS HEAD. THEY PUT A STAFF IN HIS RIGHT HAND. THEN THEY KNELT IN FRONT OF HIM AND MOCKED HIM. 'HAIL, KING OF THE JEWS!' THEY SAID. THEY SPIT ON HIM, AND TOOK THE STAFF AND STRUCK HIM ON THE HEAD AGAIN AND AGAIN.

— MATTHEW 27:27-30 NIV

Such daring mockery. Those soldiers had no idea who they were dealing with. Ten thousand angels stood ready to come to His aid. He only needed to say the word, and this obscene exhibition of human brutality would be over. Instead, He chose to bear their mockery in dignified silence: their filthy spittle, their cruelty, their ignorant laughter. Why? Because, in spite of their spiritual blindness and sin, He loved them. That doesn't make sense to our poor little minds--but from redeemed hearts it calls forth our adoration, praise and worship!

About three in the afternoon Jesus cried out in a loud voice, 'Eli, Eli, lema sabachthani?' (which means 'My God, my God, why have you forsaken me?').

— Matthew 27:46 NIV

How can we even begin to comprehend what took place in that awful moment, upon which depended our eternal salvation. What did this mean to Him who is the very image of God's substance? We can only guess at the extent of His anguish and frame it in terms of human experience: *'I am come into deep waters, where the floods overflow me.'* (Ps 69:2)

∽

'Abba, Father,' he said, 'everything is possible for you. Take this cup from me. Yet not what I will, but what you will.'

— Mark 14:36 NIV

He had just instituted the New Covenant remembrance of Himself in the upper room; yet in Gethsemane, as the reality of the bitter cup His Father had given Him to drink pressed in upon Him, *'He asked if it were possible, The cup might pass away...'* We can only ever have a superficial knowledge of His sufferings. Yet, in the full knowledge of its bitterness He said *'not what I will, but what you will'* (Mark 14:36).

∽

The Suffering of Christ

> Jesus...told them...the Son of Man...will be delivered over to the Gentiles. They will mock him, insult him and spit on him; they will flog him and kill him. On the third day he will rise again.
>
> — Luke 18:31-33 NIV)

Nothing took the Lord by surprise. He knew in exact detail how and when He would die, how men would treat Him, and that He would rise again, because our redemption was all planned out before the dawn of time.

> *Praise our God who willed it thus,*
> *Praise His Son who died for us,*
> *Praise the Father for the Son,*
> *Who so vast a work hath done.*
>
> — J. Cennick, 1718-1755
> (PHSS 23)

Trees

Like an apple tree among the trees of the forest is my beloved...I delight to sit in his shade, and his fruit is sweet to my taste.

— Song of Songs 2:3 NIV)

Unlike other trees, the apple tree produces sweet fruit. Something uniquely pleasant and good. Today we think of the tree on which our Beloved became a curse when He was 'made to be sin' on our behalf. But like the lover in the song, We have 'tasted that the LORD is gracious' and have found our eternal rest in the shade of that tree. *'...and his banner over me was love.'*

Triumph and Victory

DAVID RECOVERED EVERYTHING THE AMALEKITES
HAD TAKEN ... NOTHING WAS MISSING ... DAVID
BROUGHT EVERYTHING BACK.

— (1 SAMUEL 30:18,19 NIV

In this David is a type of the Lord Jesus Christ. Satan robbed God of the perfect communion and harmony that existed in Eden but by the blood of His atonement the Lord Jesus restored what Satan took away.

> *Final is the foes' defeat;*
> *Jesus triumphed by His power,*
> *And His triumph is complete.*
>
> — T. KELLY 1769-1854
> (PHSS 56)

Truth and Sincerity

The LORD forbid that I should give you the inheritance of my fathers.

— 1 Kings 21:3 ESV

Ahab was a profane man. To him, Naboth's vineyard was much the same as any other. But to Naboth it wasn't just any vineyard. It was a precious inheritance handed down from his forefathers and it wasn't for sale.

Jude exhorts us to *'contend earnestly for the faith'*, the body of New Testament teaching handed down from our spiritual forefathers. It is non-negotiable!

Speak the truth to each other, and render true and sound judgment in your courts; do not plot evil against each other, and do not love to swear falsely.

— Zechariah 8:16,17 NIV

In a world where truth is trampled underfoot, God's people have an obligation to stand up for what is true and right in accordance with the Word of God. If we don't do it, who will?

You are the salt of the earth.

— Matthew 5:13 NIV

Salt is a preservative. Applied to a wound it stings but helps to heal the wound. Sometimes the truth hurts. The unvarnished truth is that original sin inherited from Adam, has caused untold damage; selfishness, pride and cruelty come from within. The truth hurts but also heals. Only when we hate what we are by nature and seek God's mercy, can we experience His forgiveness.

Truth and Sincerity

> The reason I was born and came into the world is to testify to the truth. Everyone on the side of truth listens to me.
>
> — John 18:37 NIV

As disciples of the Lord Jesus Christ, we are called to stand for these unalterable truths: Jesus died for our sins; God has called us into the fellowship of His Son to worship Him in Spirit and truth; He has given detailed instructions about how to do that.

> For Christ, our Passover lamb, has been sacrificed. Therefore let us keep the Festival, not with the old bread leavened with malice and wickedness, but with the unleavened bread of sincerity and truth.
>
> — 1 Cor. 5:7,8 NIV)

Collective communion with Christ is sacred. We cannot keep His remembrance with a good conscience if we continue to practice sinful or un-Christ-like behaviour. Disciples of Christ must be honest about their motives. Our service will only be acceptable to God, if our behaviour is governed by Bible-based truth.

Unbelief

AND HE COULD DO NO MIGHTY WORK THERE, EXCEPT THAT HE LAID HIS HANDS ON A FEW SICK PEOPLE AND HEALED THEM. 6AND HE MARVELLED BECAUSE OF THEIR UNBELIEF.

— MARK 6:5,6 ESV

To have been able to say to the citizens of Nazareth, 'Your sins are forgiven', would have been a mighty, work with eternal results. What an obstacle to the entrance of God's grace is unbelief. How sad that their 'lack of faith' in Him prevented their deliverance from the power of sin.

Unity

HOW GOOD AND PLEASANT IT IS WHEN GOD'S
PEOPLE LIVE TOGETHER IN UNITY!

— PSALM 133:1 NIV

Unity is especially valuable to God. Unity without a shared vision is like a wall with a thin veneer of cement: prod it and it falls apart because it's only surface unity. Under Christ's New Covenant, Churches of God will remain united by being *'built upon the foundation of the apostles and prophets...'* (Eph. 2:20)

UNITY...IT IS LIKE PRECIOUS OIL POURED ON THE HEAD.

— PSALM 133:1-2 NIV

The oil speaks of the Holy Spirit. The Lord Jesus was anointed *'with the Holy Spirit and with power..'* (Acts 10:38) That same power united His disciples on the day of Pentecost. In the power of the Holy Spirit they turned the world upside down. Those who are filled with the Spirit are of one mind, they are united in vision and purpose in the work of their Lord.

FOR THERE THE LORD BESTOWS HIS BLESSING, EVEN LIFE FOREVERMORE.

— PSALM 133:3 NIV)

Where? The Lord Jesus bestowed redemption blessings for us outside the city wall of Zion on earth; even more so in the Zion which is above, where He is now our Great High Priest, the mediator of a New Covenant. But this takes us back to the first verse: the Lord bestows His greatest blessings in the place where Divine Unity is precious to, and practised by His friends (John 15:14).

Unity

Holy Father, protect them by the power of your name, the name you gave me, so that they may be one as we are one...May they also be in us so that the world may believe that you have sent me. I have given them the glory that you gave me, that they may be one as we are one—I in them and you in me—so that they may be brought to complete unity. Then the world will know that you sent me and have loved them even as you have loved me.

— John 17:11-23 NIV

The Lord Jesus prayed that His disciples would be one with God the Father, with Himself and with each other. Only if they were filled with, and bound together in the love of God, would the world see and know and believe in the Saviour God has sent.

Vengeance

DAVID SAID TO ABIGAIL, 'PRAISE BE TO THE LORD, THE GOD OF ISRAEL, WHO HAS SENT YOU TODAY TO MEET ME. MAY YOU BE BLESSED FOR YOUR GOOD JUDGMENT AND FOR KEEPING ME ... FROM AVENGING MYSELF ...'

— 1 SAMUEL 25:32,33 NIV

How thankful you should be that you don't need to take the law into your own hands. The LORD of the armies of Heaven is on your side. Take your concerns to Him. Let Him fight your battles for you.

WISDOM

WILL YOUR MOTHER AND I AND YOUR BROTHERS ACTUALLY COME AND BOW DOWN TO THE GROUND BEFORE YOU?' HIS BROTHERS WERE JEALOUS OF HIM, BUT HIS FATHER KEPT THE MATTER IN MIND.

— GENESIS 37:10,11 NIV

Jacob knew the significance of dreams. God had appeared to him at Bethel in an unforgettable vision of the night when he fled from Esau, and had revealed the ongoing 'two-lane' angelic traffic that occurs between heaven and earth. So Jacob, although he rebuked Joseph because the dream made no sense to him at the time, *'kept the saying in mind.'* It is good to keep the word of God in mind.

A BIBLE VERSE EACH DAY

> Wisdom is a shelter as money is a shelter, but the advantage of knowledge is this: Wisdom preserves those who have it.
>
> — Ecclesiastes 7:12 NIV

Both wisdom and wealth have a protective influence. Money may shield us from poverty in this life but its value is limited to the natural sphere. By contrast, wisdom will save us from fatal errors in every department of life. Wisdom is of spiritual and eternal value.

~

> Moses was educated in all the wisdom of the Egyptians and was powerful in speech and action.
>
> — Acts 7:22 NIV

Egypt's wisdom was limited to material and economic advancement. When it came to knowing God, the world's wisdom fell short. Moses had to learn humility for 40 years in the wilderness before God revealed himself in the burning bush. He had to unlearn the folly of human pride. he had to learn to depend on God, not on His natural abilities.

~

Wisdom

Eye has not seen, nor ear heard, Nor have entered into the heart of man The things which God has prepared for those who love Him.

— 1 Cor. 2:9 NKJV

Here Paul is writing about the wisdom that comes from above, in particular about the previously hidden depths of the master-plan of God's salvation, now revealed by the Holy Spirit to the redeemed hearts of spiritually minded people.

Do not deceive yourselves. If any of you think you are wise by the standards of this age, you should become 'fools' so that you may become wise.

— 1 Corinthians 3:18 NIV)

This doesn't mean you should turn your back on knowledge per se. It simply means that when the wisdom of this world contradicts the wisdom of God, we should reject the world's wisdom in favour of God's wisdom. Two obvious examples are moral relativism and salvation by works.

A BIBLE VERSE EACH DAY

> Look carefully (AV- circumspectly) then how you walk, not as unwise but as wise, making the best use of the time, because the days are evil.
>
> — Ephesians 5:15-16 ESV

A cat walks circumspectly when it picks its way around a puddle of water, avoiding the thing that would cause it discomfort. We also need to walk with great care, being surrounded by many potentially time-wasting hazards that would impede our spiritual progress.

Worship

YET FOR US THERE IS BUT ONE GOD, THE FATHER, FROM WHOM ALL THINGS CAME AND FOR WHOM WE LIVE; AND THERE IS BUT ONE LORD, JESUS CHRIST, THROUGH WHOM ALL THINGS CAME AND THROUGH WHOM WE LIVE.

— 1 CORINTHIANS 8:6 NIV

No matter how many religions claim to have found the answer to the moral and spiritual needs of the human heart, the Word of God teaches that there is only one true God and only one Saviour in whom we may discover life in all it's fulness.

MAKE AN ALTAR OF ACACIA WOOD FOR BURNING INCENSE ... 'AARON MUST BURN FRAGRANT INCENSE ON THE ALTAR ... SO INCENSE WILL BURN REGULARLY BEFORE THE LORD FOR THE GENERATIONS TO COME ... ONCE A YEAR AARON SHALL MAKE ATONEMENT ON ITS HORNS. THIS ANNUAL ATONEMENT MUST BE MADE WITH THE BLOOD OF THE ATONING SIN OFFERING FOR THE GENERATIONS TO COME. IT IS MOST HOLY TO THE LORD.

— EXODUS 30:1-10

Every morning and evening, the unique fragrance of that incense arose to God from the altar of incense, on which the blood of the sin-offering had been placed on the annual day of atonement; pointing forward to the fragrance of the once and for all sacrifice that the Lord Jesus would make for us on the cross of Calvary. How precious and sweet to God, is the fragrance of that sacrifice. Today, week after week, disciples of Christ, who have been added to churches of God according to the pattern given in the New Testament, are privileged to *'offer up a sacrifice of praise to God continually, that is, the fruit of lips which make confession to his name'* (Heb. 13:15 ASV).

Learn more about the Churches of God online:
https://churchesofgod.info/

THE CHIEF POINT IS THIS: WE HAVE SUCH A HIGH PRIEST, WHO SAT DOWN ON THE RIGHT HAND OF THE THRONE OF THE MAJESTY IN THE HEAVENS, A MINISTER OF THE SANCTUARY, AND OF THE TRUE TABERNACLE, WHICH THE LORD PITCHED, NOT MAN.

— HEBREWS 8:1-2 RV

There is a throne in the heavens; it is the seat of unlimited, almighty, divine power. The Lord Jesus, our high priest, sits at God's right hand, the place of highest honour. Through Him, we may enter the divine presence and enjoy communion with God, individually and collectively.

Bibliography

Fair Sunshine: Character Studies of the Scottish Covenanters. Jock Purves. Banner of Truth Trust, 1968.

In Praise of the Saviour. A collection of poems written by Ellen Jean Bairnson (1903-1975), of Brakes, Dunrossness, Shetland. (Published posthumously by her husband, Jimmy Bairnson).

Jottings. John Miller. Hayes Press.https://books2read.com/b/bQAkld

Notes on the New Testament Scriptures. John Miller. Hayes Press.https://books2read.com/rl/hayes-press/ (Scroll down this webpage to locate the series of commentaries on every book in the New Testament, by John Miller).

Psalms, Hymns and Spiritual Songs. Commonly known as the 'PHSS Hymnbook'. Needed Truth Publishing Office (now Hayes Press); for the use of the Churches of God, Revised 1971. Available online here: https://books2read.com/rl/hayes-press/ And here (scroll down to see/listen to individual hymns played on the organ):https://www.youtube.com/@theymaybeone1889/videos

Vine's Expository Dictionary of NT Words. W.E. Vine https://www.studylight.org/dictionaries/eng/ved.html

∽

About the Author

Jo Johnson is a Christian writer and artist. He lives in Fife, Scotland with his wife Norma. Jo divides his time between painting, writing and occasional grandparenting duties!

Snapshots from Memory (my autobiography) Get it here: https://mybook.to/SnapshotsEbook

Audible link: Snapshots from Memory-Audiobook

instagram.com/jojohnsonart

Also by Jo Johnson

'JOSEPH the Epic Poetic' - the Bible Story of Joseph in verse, a children's book. Available from Amazon or from any major High Street bookseller, in both paperback and Hardback.

https://mybook.to/JOSEPHTheEpicPoetic

On YouTube: Joseph The Epic Poetic! Book Reading

The Secret Diaries of Two Auld Grannies - The long-lost diaries of my great-grandmother and great-great grandmother!

https://mybook.to/GranniesDiariesPB

See all my books here: https://mybook.to/booksbyJoJohnson

www.ingramcontent.com/pod-product-compliance
Lightning Source LLC
Chambersburg PA
CBHW061743070526
44585CB00025B/2788